THE CODE OF HAMMURABI
TWO RENOWNED TRANSLATIONS

LEONARD WILLIAM KING

ROBERT FRANCIS HARPER

ALICIA EDITIONS

CONTENTS

INTRODUCTION   1
by Charles F. Horne, Ph.D.

Babylonian Law—The Code of Hammurabi   3
by the Rev. Claude Hermann Walter Johns, M.A. Litt.D.

Bibliography   23

PART ONE
TRANSLATION BY WILLIAM LEONARD KING

Hammurabi's Code of Laws   27

PART TWO
TRANSLATION BY ROBERT FRANCIS HARPER

Hammurabi's Code of Laws   59

A SECTION OF THE CODE OF HAMMURABI

INTRODUCTION
BY CHARLES F. HORNE, PH.D.

. . . [H]ammurabi] was the ruler who chiefly established the greatness of Babylon, the world's first metropolis. Many relics of Hammurabi's reign ([1795-1750 BC]) have been preserved, and today we can study this remarkable King . . . as a wise law-giver in his celebrated code. . .

. . . [B]y far the most remarkable of the Hammurabi records is his code of laws, the earliest-known example of a ruler proclaiming publicly to his people an entire body of laws, arranged in orderly groups, so that all men might read and know what was required of them. The code was carved upon a black stone monument, eight feet high, and clearly intended to be reared in public view. This noted stone was found in the year 1901, not in Babylon, but in a city of the Persian mountains, to which some later conqueror must have carried it in triumph. It begins and ends with addresses to the gods. Even a law code was in those days regarded as a subject for prayer, though the prayers here are chiefly cursings of whoever shall neglect or destroy the law.

The code then regulates in clear and definite strokes the organization of society. The judge who blunders in a law case is to be expelled from his judgeship forever, and heavily fined. The witness who testifies falsely is to be slain. Indeed, all the heavier crimes are made punishable with death. Even if a man builds a house badly, and it falls and kills the owner, the builder is to be slain. If the owner's son was killed, then the builder's son is slain. We can see where the Hebrews learned their law of "an eye for an eye." These grim retaliatory punishments take no note of excuses or explanations, but only of the fact--with one striking exception. An accused person was allowed to cast himself into "the river," the Euphrates. Apparently the art of swimming was unknown; for if the current bore him to the shore alive he was declared innocent, if he drowned he was guilty. So we learn that faith in the justice of the ruling gods was already firmly, though somewhat childishly, established in the minds of men.

Yet even with this earliest set of laws, as with most things Babylonian, we find ourselves dealing with the end of things rather than the beginnings. Hammurabi's code was not really the earliest. The preceding sets of laws have disappeared, but we have found several traces of them, and Hammurabi's own code clearly implies their existence. He is but reorganizing a legal system long established.

Charles F. Horne, Ph.D.

BABYLONIAN LAW—THE CODE OF HAMMURABI
BY THE REV. CLAUDE HERMANN WALTER JOHNS, M.A. LITT.D.

from the Eleventh Edition of the Encyclopedia Britannica, 1910-1911

The material for the study of Babylonian law is singularly extensive without being exhaustive. The so-called "contracts," including a great variety of deeds, conveyances, bonds, receipts, accounts and, most important of all, the actual legal decisions given by the judges in the law courts, exist in thousands. Historical inscriptions, royal charters and rescripts, despatches, private letters and the general literature afford welcome supplementary information. Even grammatical and lexicographical works, intended solely to facilitate the study of ancient literature, contain many extracts or short sentences bearing on law and custom. The so-called "Sumerian Family Laws" are thus preserved. The discovery of the now celebrated Code of Hammurabi (hereinafter simply termed the Code) has, however, made a more systematic study possible than could have resulted from the classification and interpretation of the other material. Some fragments of a later code exist and have been published; but there still remain many points upon which we have no evidence.

This material dates from the earliest times down to the

commencement of our era. The evidence upon a particular point may be very full at one period and almost entirely lacking at another. The Code forms the backbone of the skeleton sketch which is here reconstructed. The fragments of it which have been recovered from Assur-bani-pal's library at Nineveh and later Babylonian copies show that it was studied, divided into chapters entitled Ninu ilu sirum from its opening words, and recopied for fifteen hundred years or more. The greater part of It remained in force, even through the Persian, Greek and Parthian conquests, which affected private life in Babylonia very little, and it survived to influence Syro-Roman and later Mahommedan law in Mesopotamia. The law and custom which preceded the Code we shall call "early," that of the New Babylonian empire (as well as the Persian, Greek, &c.) "late." The law in Assyria was derived from Babylonia but conserved early features long after they had disappeared elsewhere.

When the Semitic tribes settled in the cities of Babylonia, their tribal custom passed over into city law. The early history of the country is the story of a struggle for supremacy between the cities. A metropolis demanded tribute and military support from its subject cities but left their local cults and customs unaffected. The city rights and usages were respected by kings and conquerors alike.

As late as the accession of Assur-bani-pal and Samas-sum-yukin we find the Babylonians appealing to their city laws that groups of aliens to the number of twenty at a time were free to enter the city, that foreign women once married to Babylonian husbands could not be enslaved and that not even a dog that entered the city could be put to death untried.

The population of Babylonia was of many races from early times and intercommunication between the cities was incessant. Every city had a large number of resident aliens. This freedom of intercourse must have tended to assimilate custom. It was, however, reserved for the genius of Hammurabi to make Babylon his metropolis and weld together his vast empire by a uniform system of law.

Almost all trace of tribal custom has already disappeared from the law of the Code. It is state-law; - alike self-help, blood-feud, marriage by capture, are absent; though family solidarity, district responsibility, ordeal, the lex talionis, are primitive features that remain. The king is a benevolent autocrat, easily accessible to all his subjects, both able and willing to protect the weak against the highest-placed oppressor. The royal power, however, can only pardon when private resentment is appeased. The judges are strictly supervised and appeal is allowed. The whole land is covered with feudal holdings, masters of the levy, police, &c. There is a regular postal system. The pax Babylonica is so assured that private individuals do not hesitate to ride in their carriage from Babylon to the coast of the Mediterranean. The position of women is free and dignified.

The Code did not merely embody contemporary custom or conserve ancient law. It is true that centuries of law-abiding and litigious habitude had accumulated in the temple archives of each city vast stores of precedent in ancient deeds and the records of judicial decisions, and that intercourse had assimilated city custom. The universal habit of writing and perpetual recourse to written contract even more modified primitive custom and ancient precedent. Provided the parties could agree, the Code left them free to contract as a rule. Their deed of agreement was drawn up in the temple by a notary public, and confirmed by an oath "by god and the king." It was publicly sealed and witnessed by professional witnesses, as well as by collaterally interested parties. The manner in which it was thus executed may have been sufficient security that its stipulations were not impious or illegal. Custom or public opinion doubtless secured that the parties would not agree to wrong. In case of dispute the judges dealt first with the contract. They might not sustain it, but if the parties did not dispute it, they were free to observe it. The judges' decision might, however, be appealed against. Many contracts contain the proviso that in case of future dispute the parties would abide by "the decision of the king." The Code made known, in a vast number of cases, what that decision would be, and many cases of appeal to the king were sent back to the judges with orders to decide in accordance with it. The Code itself was carefully and logically arranged and the order of its sections was conditioned by their subject-matter. Nevertheless the order is not that of modern scientific treatises, and a somewhat different order from both is most convenient for our purpose.

The Code contemplates the whole population as falling into

three classes, the amelu, the muskinu and the ardu. The amelu was a patrician, the man of family, whose birth, marriage and death were registered, of ancestral estates and full civil rights. He had aristocratic privileges and responsibilities, the right to exact retaliation for corporal injuries, and liability to heavier punishment for crimes and misdemeanours, higher fees and fines to pay. To this class belonged the king and court, the higher officials, the professions and craftsmen. The term became in time a mere courtesy title but originally carried with it standing. Already in the Code, when status is not concerned, it is used to denote "any one." There was no property qualification nor does the term appear to be racial. It is most difficult to characterize the muskinu exactly. The term came in time to mean "a beggar" and with that meaning has passed through Aramaic and Hebrew into many modern languages; but though the Code does not regard him as necessarily poor, he may have been landless. He was free, but had to accept monetary compensation for corporal injuries, paid smaller fees and fines, even paid less offerings to the gods. He inhabited a separate quarter of the city. There is no reason to regard him as specially connected with the court, as a royal pensioner, nor as forming the bulk of the population. The rarity of any reference to him in contemporary documents makes further specification conjectural. The ardu was a slave, his master's chattel, and formed a very numerous class. He could acquire property and even hold other slaves. His master clothed and fed him, paid his doctor's fees, but took all compensation paid for injury done to him. His master usually found him a slave-girl as wife (the children were then born slaves), often set him up in a house (with farm or business) and simply took an annual rent of him. Otherwise he might marry a freewoman (the children were then free), who might bring him a dower which his master could not touch, and at his death one-half of his property passed to his master as his heir. He could acquire his freedom by purchase from his master, or might be freed and dedicated to a temple, or even adopted, when he became an amelu and not a muskinu. Slaves were recruited by purchase abroad, from captives taken in war and by freemen degraded for debt or crime. A slave often ran away; if caught, the captor was bound to restore him to his master, and the Code fixes a reward of two shekels which the owner must pay the captor. It was about one-tenth of the average value. To detain, harbour, &c., a slave was punished by death. So was an attempt to get him to leave the city. A slave bore an identification mark, which could only be removed by a surgical operation and which later consisted of his owner's name tattooed or branded on the arm. On the great estates in Assyria and its subject provinces were many serfs, mostly of subject race, settled captives, or quondam slaves, tied to the soil they cultivated and sold with the estate but capable of possessing land and property of their own. There is little trace of serfs in Babylonia, unless the muskinu be really a serf.

The god of a city was originally owner of its land, which encircled it with an inner ring of irrigable arable land and an outer fringe of pasture, and the citizens were his tenants. The god and his viceregent, the king, had long ceased to disturb tenancy, and were content with fixed dues in naturalia, stock, money or service. One of the earliest monuments records the purchase by a king of a large estate for his son, paying a fair market price and adding a handsome honorarium to the many owners in costly garments, plate, and precious articles of furniture. The Code recognizes complete private ownership in land, but apparently extends the right to hold land to votaries, merchants (and resident aliens?). But all land was sold subject to its fixed charges. The king, however, could free land from these charges by charter, which was a frequent way of rewarding those who deserved well of the state. It is from these charters that we learn nearly all we know of the obligations that lay upon land. The state demanded men for the army and the corvee as well as dues in kind. A definite area was bound to find a bowman together with his linked pikeman (who bore the shield for both) and to furnish them with supplies for the campaign. This area was termed "a bow" as early as the 8th century B.C., but the usage was much earlier. Later, a horseman was due from certain areas. A man was only bound to serve so many (six?) times, but the land had to find a man annually. The service was usually discharged by slaves and serfs, but the amelu (and perhaps the muskenu) went to war. The "bows" were grouped in tens and hundreds. The corvee was less regular. The letters of Hammurabi often deal with claims to exemption. Religious officials and shepherds in charge of flocks were exempt. Special liabilities lay upon riparian owners to repair canals, bridges, quays, &c. The state claimed certain proportions of all crops, stock, &c. The king's messengers could commandeer any subject's property, giving a receipt. Further, every city had its own octroi duties, customs, ferry dues, highway and water rates. The king had long ceased to be, if he ever was, owner of the land. He had his own royal estates, his private property and dues from all his subjects. The higher officials had endowments and official residences. The Code regulates the feudal position of certain classes. They held an estate from the king consisting of house, garden, field, stock and a salary, on condition of personal service on the king's errand. They could not delegate the service on pain of death. When ordered abroad they could nominate a son, if capable, to hold the benefice and carry on the duty. If there was no son capable, the state put in a locum tenens, but granted one-third to the wife to maintain herself and children. The benefice was inalienable, could not be sold, pledged, exchanged, sublet, devised or diminished. Other land was held of the state for rent. Ancestral estate was strictly tied to the family. If a holder would sell, the family had the right of redemption and there seems to have been no time-limit to its exercise.

The temple occupied a most important position. It received from its estates, from tithes and other fixed dues, as well as from the sacrifices (a customary share) and other offerings of the faithful, vast amounts of all sorts of naturalia; besides money and permanent gifts. The larger temples had many officials and servants. Originally, perhaps, each town clustered round one temple, and each head of a family had a right to minister there and share its receipts. As the city grew, the right to so many days a year at one or other shrine (or its "gate") descended in certain families and became a species of property which could be pledged, rented or shared within the family, but not alienated. In spite of all these demands, however, the temples became great granaries and store-houses; as they also were the city archives. The temple held its responsibilities. If a citizen was captured by the enemy and could not ransom himself the temple of his city must do so. To the temple came the poor farmer to borrow seed corn or supplies for harvesters, &c.--advances which he repaid without interest. The king's power over the temple was not proprietary but administrative. He might borrow from it but repaid like other borrowers. The tithe seems to have been the composition for the rent due to the god for his land. It is not clear that all lands paid tithe, perhaps only such as once had a special connexion with the temple.

The Code deals with a class of persons devoted to the service of a god, as vestals or hierodules. The vestals were vowed to chastity, lived together in a great nunnery, were forbidden to open or enter a tavern, and together with other votaries had many privileges.

The Code recognizes many ways of disposing of property--sale, lease, barter, gift, dedication, deposit, loan, pledge, all of which were matters of contract. Sale was the delivery of the purchase (in the case of real estate symbolized by a staff, a key, or deed of conveyance) in return for the purchase money, receipts being given for both. Credit, if given, was treated as a debt, and secured as a loan by the seller to be repaid by the buyer, fr which he gave a bond. The Code admits no claim unsubstantiated by documents or the oath of witnesses. A buyer had to convince himself of the seller's title. If he bought (or received on deposit) from a minor or a slave without power of attorney, he would be executed as a thief. If the goods were stolen and the rightful owner reclaimed them, he had to prove his purchase by producing the seller and the deed of sale or witnesses to it. Otherwise he would be adjudged a thief and die. If he proved his purchase, he had to give up the property but had his remedy against the seller or, if he had died, could reclaim five-fold from his estate. A man who bought a slave abroad, might find that he had been stolen or captured from Babylonia, and he had to restore him to his former owner without profit. If he bought property belonging to a feudal holding, or to a ward in chancery, he had to return it and forfeit what he gave for it as well. He could repudiate the purchase of a slave attacked by the bennu sickness within the month (later, a hundred days), and had a female slave three days on approval. A defect of title or undisclosed liability would invalidate the sale at any time.

Landowners frequently cultivated their land themselves but might employ a husbandman or let it. The husbandman was bound to carry out the proper cultivation, raise an average crop and leave the field in good tilth. In case the crop failed the Code fixed a statutory return. Land might be let at a fixed rent when the Code enacted that accidental loss fell on the tenant. If let on share-profit, the landlord and tenant shared the loss proportionately to their stipulated share of profit. If the tenant paid his rent and left the land in good tilth, the landlord could not interfere nor forbid subletting. Waste land was let to reclaim, the tenant being rent-free for three years and paying a stipulated rent in the fourth year. If the tenant neglected to reclaim the land the Code enacted that he must hand it over in good tilth and fixed a statutory rent. Gardens or plantations were let in the same ways and under the same conditions; but for date-groves four years' free tenure was allowed. The metayer system was in vogue, especially on temple lands. The landlord found land, labour, oxen for ploughing and working the watering-machines, carting, threshing or other implements, seed corn, rations for the workmen and fodder for the cattle. The tenant, or steward, usually had other land of his own. If he stole the seed, rations or fodder, the Code enacted that his fingers should be cut off. If he appropriated or sold the implements, impoverished or sublet the cattle, he was heavily fined and in default of payment might be condemned to be torn to pieces by the cattle on the field. Rent was as contracted.

Irrigation was indispensable. If the irrigator neglected to repair his dyke, or left his runnel open and caused a flood, he had to make good the damage done to his neighbours' crops, or be sold with his family to pay the cost. The theft of a watering-machine, water-bucket or other agricultural implement was heavily fined.

Houses were let usually for the year, but also for longer terms, rent being paid in advance, half-yearly. The contract generally specified that the house was in good repair, and the tenant was bound to keep it so. The woodwork, including doors and door frames, was removable, and the tenant might bring and take away his own. The Code enacted that if the landlord would re-enter before the term was up, he must remit a fair proportion of the rent. Land was leased for houses or other buildings to be built upon it, the tenant being rent-free for eight or ten years; after which the building came into the landlord's possession.

Despite the multitude of slaves, hired labour was often needed, especially at harvest. This was matter of contract, and the hirer, who usually paid in advance, might demand a guarantee to fulfil the engagement. Cattle were hired for ploughing, working the watering-machines, carting, threshing, etc. The Code fixed a statutory wage for sowers, ox-drivers, field-labourers, and hire for oxen, asses, &c.

There were many herds and flocks. The flocks were committed to a shepherd who gave receipt for them and took them out to pasture. The Code fixed him a wage. He was responsible for all care, must restore ox for ox, sheep for sheep, must breed them satisfactorily. Any dishonest use of the flock had to be repaid ten-fold, but loss by disease or wild beasts fell on the owner. The shepherd made good all loss due to his neglect. If he let the flock feed on a field of corn he had to pay damages four-fold; if he turned them into standing corn when they ought to have been folded he paid twelve-fold.

In commercial matters, payment in kind was still common, though the contracts usually stipulate for cash, naming the standard expected, that of Babylon, Larsa, Assyria, Carchemish, &c. The Code enacted, however, that a debtor must be allowed to pay in produce according to statutory scale. If a debtor had neither money nor crop, the creditor-must not refuse goods.

Debt was secured on the person of the debtor. Distraint on a debtor's corn was forbidden by the Code; not only must the creditor give it back, but his illegal action forfeited his claim altogether. An unwarranted seizure for debt was fined, as was the distraint of a working ox. The debtor being seized for debt could nominate as mancipium or hostage to work off the debt, his wife, a child, or slave. The creditor could only hold a wife or child three years as mancipium. If the mancipium died a natural death while in the creditor's possession no claim could lie against the latter; but if he was the cause of death by cruelty, he had to give son for son, or pay for a slave. He could sell a slave-hostage, unless she were a slave-girl who had borne her master children. She had to be redeemed by her owner.

The debtor could also pledge his property, and in contracts often pledged a field house or crop. The Code enacted, however, that the debtor should always take the crop himself and pay the creditor from it. If the crop failed, payment was deferred and no interest could be charged for that year. If the debtor did not cultivate the field himself he had to pay for the cultivation, but if the cultivation was already finished he must harvest it himself and pay his debt from the crop. If the cultivator did not get a crop this would not cancel his contract. Pledges were often made where the intrinsic value of the article was equivalent to the amount of the debt; but antichretic pledge was more common, where the profit of the pledge was a set-off against the interest of the debt. The whole property of the debtor might be pledged as security for the payment of the debt, without any of it coming into the enjoyment of the creditor. Personal guarantees were often given that the debtor would repay or the guarantor become liable himself.

Trade was very extensive. A common way of doing business was for a merchant to entrust goods or money to a travelling agent, who sought a market for his goods. The caravans travelled far beyond the limits of the empire. The Code insisted that the agent should inventory and give a receipt for all that he received. No claim could be made for anything not so entered. Even if the agent made no profit he was bound to return double what he had received, if he made poor profit he had to make up the deficiency; but he was not responsible for loss by robbery or extortion on his travels. On his return, the principal must give a receipt for what was handed over to him. Any false entry or claim on the agent's part was penalised three-fold, on the principal's part six-fold. In normal cases profits were divided according to contract, usually equally.

A considerable amount of forwarding was done by the caravans. The carrier gave a receipt for the consignment, took all responsibility and exacted a receipt on delivery. If he defaulted he paid five-fold. He was usually paid in advance. Deposit, especially warehousing of grain, was charged for at one-sixtieth. The warehouseman took all risks, paid double for all shortage, but no claim could be made unless be had given a properly witnessed receipt. Water traffic on the Euphrates and canals was early very considerable. Ships, whose tonnage was estimated at the amount of grain they could carry, were continually hired for the a transport of all kinds of goods. The Code fixes the price for building and insists on the builder's giving a year's guarantee of seaworthiness. It fixes the hire of ship and of crew. The captain was responsible for the freight and the ship; he had to replace all loss. Even if he refloated the ship he had to pay a fine of half its value for sinking it. In the case of collision the boat under way was responsible for damages to the boat at anchor. The Code also regulated the liquor traffic, fixing a fair price for beer and forbidding the connivance of the tavern-keeper (a female!) at disorderly conduct or treasonable assembly, under pain of death. She was to hale the offenders to the palace, which implied an efficient and accessible police system.

Payment through a banker or by written draft against deposit was frequent. Bonds to pay were treated as negotiable. Interest a was rarely charged on advances by the temple or wealthy land-owners for pressing needs, but this may have been part of the metayer system. The borrowers may have been tenants. Interest was charged at very high rates for overdue loans of this kind. Merchants (and even temples in some cases) made ordinary business loans, charging from 20 to 30%.

Marriage retained the form of purchase, but was essentially a contract to be man and wife together. The marriage of young people was usually arranged between the relatives, the bride- groom's father providing the bride-price, which with other presents the suitor ceremonially presented to the bride's father. This bride-price was usually handed over by her father to the bride on her marriage, and so came back into the bridegroom's possession, along with her dowry, which was her portion as a daughter. The bride-price varied much, according to the position of the parties, but was in excess of that paid for a slave. The Code enacted that if the father does not, after accepting a man's presents, give him his daughter, he, must return the presents doubled. Even if his decision was brought about by libel on the part of the suitor's friend this was done, and the Code enacted that the faithless friend should not marry the girl. If a suitor changed his mind, he forfeited the presents. The dowry might include real estate, but generally consisted of personal effects and household furniture. It remained the wife's for life, descending to her children, if any; otherwise returning to her family, when the husband could deduct the bride-price if it had not been given to her, or return it, if it had. The marriage ceremony included joining of hands and the utterance of some formula of acceptance on the part of the bridegroom, as "I am the son of nobles, silver and gold shall fill thy lap, thou shalt be my wife, I will be thy husband. Like the fruit of a garden I will give thee offspring." It must be performed by a freeman.

The marriage contract, without which the Code ruled that the woman was no wife, usually stated the consequences to which each party was liable for repudiating the other. These by no means necessarily agree with the Code. Many conditions might be inserted: as that the wife should act as maidservant to her mother-in-law, or to a first wife. The married couple formed a unit as to external responsibility, especially for debt. The man was responsible for debts contracted by his wife, even before her marriage, as well as for his own; but he could use her as a mancipium. Hence the Code allowed a proviso to be inserted in the marriage contract, that the wife should not be seized for her husband's prenuptial debts; but enacted that then he was not responsible for her prenuptial debts, and, in any case, that both together were responsible for all debts contracted after marriage. A man might make his wife a settlement by deed of gift, which gave her a life interest in part of his property, and he might reserve to her the right to bequeath it to a favourite child, but she could in no case leave it to her family. Although married she always remained a member of her father's house--she is rarely named wife of A, usually daughter of B, or mother of C.

Divorce was optional with the man, but he had to restore the dowry and, if the wife had borne him children, she had the custody of them. He had then to assign her the income of field, or garden, as well as goods, to maintain herself and children until they grew up. She then shared equally with them in the allowance (and apparently in his estate at his death) and was free to marry again. If she had no children, he returned her the dowry and paid her a sum equivalent to the bride-price, or a mina of silver, if there had been none. The latter is the forfeit usually named in the contract for his repudiation of her.

If she had been a bad wife, the Code allowed him to send her away, while he kept the children and her dowry; or he could degrade her to the position of a slave in his own house, where she would have food and clothing. She might bring an action against him for cruelty and neglect and, if she proved her case, obtain a judicial separation, taking with her her dowry. No other punishment fell on the man. If she did not prove her case, but proved to be a bad wife, she was drowned. If she were left without maintenance during her husband's involuntary absence, she could cohabit with another man, but must return to her husband if he came back, the children of the second union remaining with their own father. If she had maintenance, a breach of the marriage tie was adultery. Wilful desertion by, or exile of, the husband dissolved the marriage, and if he came back he had no claim on her property; possibly not on his own.

As a widow, the wife took her husband's place in the family, living on in his house and bringing up the children. She could only remarry with judicial consent, when the judge was bound to inventory the deceased's estate and hand it over to her and her new husband in trust for the children. They could not alienate a single utensil. If she did not remarry, she lived on in her husband's house and took a child's share on the division of his estate, when the children had grown up. She still retained her dowry and any settlement deeded to her by her husband. This property came to her children. If she had remarried, all her children shared equally in her dowry, but the first husband's gift fell to his children or to her selection among them, if so empowered.

Monogamy was the rule, and a childless wife might give her husband a maid (who was no wife) to bear him children, who were reckoned hers. She remained mistress of her maid and might degrade her to slavery again for insolence, but could not sell her if she had borne her husband children. If the wife did this, the Code did not allow the husband to take a concubine. If she would not, he could do so. The concubine was a wife, though not of the same rank; the first wife had no power over her. A concubine was a free woman, was often dowered for marriage and her children were legitimate. She could only be divorced on the same conditions as a wife. If a wife became a chronic invalid, the husband was bound to maintain her in the home they bad made together, unless she preferred to take her dowry and go back to her father's house; but he was free to remarry. In all these cases the children were legitimate and legal heirs.

There was, of course, no hindrance to a man having children by a slave girl. These children were free, in any case, and their mother could not be sold, though she might be pledged, and she was free on her master's death. These children could be legitimized by their father's acknowledgment before witnesses, and were often adopted. They then ranked equally in sharing their father's estate, but if not adopted, the wife's children divided and took first choice.

Vestal virgins were not supposed to have children, yet they could and often did marry. The Code contemplated that such a wife would give a husband a maid as above. Free women might marry slaves and be dowered for the marriage. The children were free, and at the slave's death the wife took her dowry and half what she and her husband had acquired in wedlock for self and children; the master taking the other half as his slave's heir.

A father had control over his children till their marriage. He had a right to their labour in return for their keep. He might hire them out and receive their wages, pledge them for debt, even sell them outright. Mothers had the same rights in the absence of the father; even elder brothers when both parents were dead. A father had no claim on his married children for support, but they retained a right to inherit on his death.

The daughter was not only in her father's power to be given in marriage, but he might dedicate her to the service of some god as a vestal or a hierodule; or give her as a concubine. She had no choice in these matters, which were often decided in her childhood. A grown-up daughter might wish to become a votary, perhaps in preference to an uncongenial marriage, and it seems that her father could not refuse her wish. In all these cases the father might dower her. If he did not, on his death the brothers were bound to do so, giving her a full child's share if a wife, a concubine or a vestal, but one-third of a child's share if she were a hierodule or a Marduk priestess. The latter had the privilege of exemption from state dues and absolute disposal of her property. All other daughters had only a life interest in their dowry, which reverted to their family, if childless, or went to their children if they had any. A father might, however, execute a deed granting a daughter power to leave her property to a favourite brother or sister. A daughter's estate was usually managed for her by her brothers, but if they did not satisfy her, she could appoint a steward. If she married, her husband managed it.

The son also appears to have received his share on marriage, but did not always then leave his father's house; he might bring his wife there. This was usual in child marriages.

Adoption was very common, especially where the father (or mother) was childless or had seen all his children grow up and marry away. The child was then adopted to care for the parents' old age. This was done by contract, which usually specified what the parent had to leave and what maintenance was expected. The real children, if any, were usually consenting parties to an arrangement which cut off their expectations. They even, in some cases, found the estate for the adopted child who was to relieve them of a care. If the adopted child failed to carry out the filial duty the contract was annulled in the law courts. Slaves were often adopted and if they proved unfilial were reduced to slavery again.

A craftsman often adopted a son to learn the craft. He profited by the son's labour. If he failed to teach his son the craft, that son could prosecute him and get the contract annulled. This was a form of apprenticeship, and it is not clear that the apprentice had any filial relation.

A man who adopted a son, and afterwards married and had a family of his own, could dissolve the contract but must give the adopted child one-third of a child's share in goods, but no real estate. That could only descend in the family to which he had ceased to belong. Vestals frequently adopted daughters, usually other vestals, to care for their old age.

Adoption had to be with consent of the real parents, who usually executed a deed making over the child, who thus ceased to have any claim upon them. But vestals, hierodules, certain palace officials and slaves had no rights over their children and could raise no obstacle. Foundlings and illegitimate children had no parents to object. If the adopted child discovered his true parents and wanted to return to them, his eye or tongue was torn out. An adopted child was a full heir, the contract might even assign him the position of eldest son. Usually he was residuary legatee.

All legitimate children shared equally in the father's estate at his death, reservation being made of a bride-price for an unmarried son, dower for a daughter or property deeded to favourite children by the father. There was no birthright attaching to the position of eldest son, but he usually acted as executor and after considering what each had already received equalized the shares. He even made grants in excess to the others from his own share. When there were two mothers, the two families shared equally in the father's estate until later times when the first family took two-thirds. Daughters, in the absence of sons, had sons' rights. Children also shared their own mother's property, but had no share in that of a stepmother.

A father could disinherit a son in early times without restriction, but the Code insisted upon judicial consent and that only for repeated unfilial conduct. In early times the son who denied his father had his front hair shorn, a slave-mark put on him, and could be sold as a slave; while if he denied his mother he had his front hair shorn, was driven round the city as an example and expelled his home, but not degraded to slavery.

Adultery was punished with the death of both parties by drowning, but if the husband was willing to pardon his wife, the king might intervene to pardon the paramour. For incest with his own mother, both were burned to death; with a stepmother, the man was disinherited; with a daughter, the man was exiled; with a daughter-in-law, he was drowned; with a son's betrothed, he was fined. A wife who for her lover's sake procured her husband's death was gibbeted. A betrothed girl, seduced by her prospective father-in-law, took her dowry and returned to her family, and was free to marry as she chose.

In the criminal law the ruling principle was the lex talionis. Eye for eye, tooth for tooth, limb for limb was the penalty for assault upon an amelu. A sort of symbolic retaliation was the punishment of the offending member, seen in the cutting off the hand that struck a father or stole a trust; in cutting off the breast of a wet-nurse who substituted a changeling for the child entrusted to her; in the loss of the tongue that denied father or mother (in the Elamite contracts the same penalty was inflicted for perjury); in the loss of the eye that pried into forbidden secrets. The loss of the surgeon's hand that caused loss of life or limb or the brander's hand that obliterated a slave's identification mark, are very similar. The slave, who struck a freeman or denied his master, lost an ear, the organ of hearing and symbol of obedience. To bring another into danger of death by false accusation was punished by death. To cause loss of liberty or property by false witness was punished by the penalty the perjurer sought to bring upon another.

The death penalty was freely awarded for theft and other crimes regarded as coming under that head, for theft involving entrance of palace or temple treasury, for illegal purchase from minor or slave, for selling stolen goods or receiving the same, for common theft in the open (in default of multiple restoration) or receiving the same, for false claim to goods, for kidnapping, for assisting or harbouring fugitive slaves, for detaining or appropriating same, for brigandage, for fraudulent sale of drink, for disorderly conduct of tavern, for delegation of personal service, for misappropriating the levy, for oppression of feudal holders, for causing death of a householder by bad building. The manner of death is not specified in these cases. This death penalty was also fixed for such conduct as placed another in danger of death. A specified form of death penalty occurs in the following cases:-gibbeting (on the spot where crime was committed) for burglary, later also for encroaching on the king's highway, for getting a slave-brand obliterated, for procuring husband's death; burning for incest with own mother, for vestal entering or opening tavern, for theft at fire (on the spot); drowning for adultery, rape of betrothed maiden, bigamy, bad conduct as wife, seduction of daughter-in-law.

A curious extension of the talio is the death of creditor's son for his father's having caused the death of debtor's son as mancipium; of builder's son for his father's causing the death of house-owner's son by building the house badly; the death of a man's daughter because her father caused the death of another man's daughter.

The contracts naturally do not concern such criminal cases as the above, as a rule, but marriage contracts do specify death by strangling, drowning, precipitation from a tower or pinnacle of the temple or by the iron sword for a wife's repudiation of her husband. We are quite without evidence as to the executive in all these cases.

Exile was inflicted for incest with a daughter; disinheritance for incest with a stepmother or for repeated unfilial conduct. Sixty strokes of an ox-hide scourge were awarded for a brutal assault on a superior, both being amelu. Branding (perhaps the equivalent of degradation to slavery) was the penalty for slander of a married woman or vestal. Deprivation of office in perpetuity fell upon the corrupt judge. Enslavement befell the extravagant wife and unfilial children. Imprisonment was common, but is not recognized by the Code.

The commonest of all penalties was a fine. This is awarded by the Code for corporal injuries to a muskinu or slave (paid to his master); for damages done to property, for breach of contract. The restoration of goods appropriated, illegally bought or damaged by neglect, was usually accompanied by a fine, giving it the form of multiple restoration. This might be double, treble, fourfold, fivefold, sixfold, tenfold, twelvefold, even thirtyfold, according to the enormity of the offence.

The Code recognized the importance of intention. A man who killed another in a quarrel must swear he did not do so intentionally, and was then only fined according to the rank of the deceased. The Code does not say what would be the penalty of murder, but death is so often awarded where death is caused that we can hardly doubt that the murderer was put to death. If the assault only led to injury and was unintentional, the assailant in a quarrel had to pay the doctor's fees. A brander, induced to remove a slave's identification mark, could swear to his ignorance and was free. The owner of an ox which gored a man on the street was only responsible for damages if, the ox was known by him to be vicious, even if it caused death. If the mancipium died a natural death under the creditor's hand, the creditor was scot free. In ordinary cases responsibility was not demanded for accident or for more than proper care. Poverty excused bigamy on the part of a deserted wife.

On the other hand carelessness and neglect were severely punished, as in the case of the unskilful physician, if it led to loss of life or limb his hands were cut off, a slave had to be replaced, the loss of his eye paid for to half his value; a veterinary surgeon who caused the death of an ox or ass paid quarter value; a builder, whose careless workmanship caused death, lost his life or paid for it by the death of his child, replaced slave or goods, and in any case had to rebuild the house or make good any damages due to defective building and repair the defect as well. The boat-builder had to make good any defect of construction or damage due to it for a year's warranty.

Throughout the Code respect is paid to status.

Suspicion was not enough. The criminal must be taken in the act, e.g. the adulterer, ravisher, &c. A man could not be convicted of theft unless the goods were found in his possession.

In the case of a lawsuit the plaintiff preferred his own plea. There is no trace of professional advocates, but the plea had to be in writing and the notary doubtless assisted in the drafting of it. The judge saw the plea, called the other parties before him and sent for the witnesses. If these were not at hand he might adjourn the case for their production, specifying a time up to six months. Guarantees might be entered into to produce the witnesses on a fixed day. The more important cases, especially those involving life and death, were tried by a bench of judges. With the judges were associated a body of elders, who shared in the decision, but whose exact function is not yet clear. Agreements, declarations and non-contentious cases are usually witnessed by one judge and twelve elders.

Parties and witnesses were put on oath. The penalty for the false witness was usually that which would have been awarded the convicted criminal. In matters beyond the knowledge of men, as the guilt or innocence of an alleged wizard or a suspected wife, the ordeal by water was used. The accused jumped into the sacred river, and the innocent swam while the guilty drowned. The accused could clear himself by oath where his own knowledge was alone available. The plaintiff could swear to his loss by brigands, as to goods claimed, the price paid for a slave purchased abroad or the sum due to him. But great stress was laid on the production of written evidence. It was a serious thing to lose a document. The judges might be satisfied of its existence and terms by the evidence of the witnesses to it, and then issue an order that whenever found it should be given up. Contracts annulled were ordered to be broken. The court might go a journey to view the property and even take with them the sacred symbols on which oath was made.

The decision given was embodied in writing, sealed and witnessed by the judges, the elders, witnesses and a scribe. Women might act in all these capacities. The parties swore an oath, embodied in the document, to observe its stipulations. Each took a copy and one was held by the scribe to be stored in the archives.

Appeal to the king was allowed and is well attested. The judges at Babylon seem to have formed a superior court to those of provincial towns, but a defendant might elect to answer the charge before the local court and refuse to plead at Babylon.

Finally, it may be noted that many immoral acts, such as the use of false weights, lying, &c., which could not be brought into court, are severely denounced in the Omen Tablets as likely to bring the offender into "the hand of God" as opposed to "the hand of the king."

BIBLIOGRAPHY

Contracts in general: Oppert and Menant, Documents juridiques de l'Assyrie et de la Chaldee (Paris, 1877); J. Kohler and F. E. Peiser, Aus dem Babylonischen Rechtsleben (Leipzig, 1890 ff.); F. E. Peiser, Babylonische Vertrage (Berlin, 1890), Keilinschrifiliche Actenstucke (Berlin, 1889); Br. Meissner, Beitrage zur altbabylonischen Privatrecht (Leipzig, 1893); F. E. Peiser, "Texte juristischen und geschaftlichen Inhalts," vol. iv. of Schrader's Keilinschriftliche Bibliothek (Berlin, 1896); C. H. W. Johns, Assyrian Deeds and Documents relating to the Transfer of Property (3 vols., Cambridge, 1898); H. Radau, Early Babylonian History (New York, 1900); C. H. W. Johns, Babylonian and Assyrian Laws, Contracts and Letters (Edinburgh, 1904).

For editions of texts and the innumerable articles in scientific journals see the bibliographies and references in the above works. "The Code of Hammurabi," Editio princeps, by V. Scheil in tome iv. of the Textes Elamites-Semitiques of the Memoires de la delegation en Perse (Paris, 1902); H. Winckler, "Die Gesetze Hammurabis Konigs von Babylon um 2250 v. Chr." Der alte Orient, iv. Jahrgang, Heft 4; D. H. Muller, Die Gesetze Hammurabis (Vienna, 1903); J. Kohler and F. E. Peiser, Hammurabis Gesetz (Leipzig, 1904); R. F. Harper, The Code of Hammurabi, King, of Babylon about 2250 B.C. (Chicago, 1904); S. A. Cook, The Laws of Moses and the Code of Hammurabi (London, 1903).

Rev. Claude Hermann Walter Johns, M.A. Litt.D. Master of St. Catharine's College, Cambridge. Lecturer in Assyriology, Queens' College, Cambridge, and King's College, London. Author of Assyrian Deeds and Documents of the 7th Century B.C.; The Oldest Code of Laws; Babylonian and Assyrian Laws; Contracts and Letters; etc.

PART ONE
TRANSLATION BY WILLIAM LEONARD KING

Photo of the discovery of Hammurabi's code stele, 1901.

HAMMURABI'S CODE OF LAWS

Prologue

When Anu the Sublime, King of the Anunaki, and Bel, the lord of Heaven and earth, who decreed the fate of the land, assigned to Marduk, the over-ruling son of Ea, God of righteousness, dominion over earthly man, and made him great among the Igigi, they called Babylon by his illustrious name, made it great on earth, and founded an everlasting kingdom in it, whose foundations are laid so solidly as those of heaven and earth; then Anu and Bel called by name me, Hammurabi, the exalted prince, who feared God, to bring about the rule of righteousness in the land, to destroy the wicked and the evil-doers; so that the strong should not harm the weak; so that I should rule over the black-headed people like Shamash, and enlighten the land, to further the well-being of mankind.

Hammurabi, the prince, called of Bel am I, making riches and increase, enriching Nippur and Dur-ilu beyond compare, sublime patron of E-kur; who reestablished Eridu and purified the worship of E-apsu; who conquered the four quarters of the world, made great the name of Babylon, rejoiced the heart of Marduk, his lord who daily pays his devotions in Saggil; the royal scion whom Sin made;

who enriched Ur; the humble, the reverent, who brings wealth to Gish-shir-gal; the white king, heard of Shamash, the mighty, who again laid the foundations of Sippara; who clothed the gravestones of Malkat with green; who made E-babbar great, which is like the heavens, the warrior who guarded Larsa and renewed E-babbar, with Shamash as his helper; the lord who granted new life to Uruk, who brought plenteous water to its inhabitants, raised the head of E-anna, and perfected the beauty of Anu and Nana; shield of the land, who reunited the scattered inhabitants of Isin; who richly endowed E-gal-mach; the protecting king of the city, brother of the god Zamama; who firmly founded the farms of Kish, crowned E-me-te-ursag with glory, redoubled the great holy treasures of Nana, managed the temple of Harsag-kalama; the grave of the enemy, whose help brought about the victory; who increased the power of Cuthah; made all glorious in E-shidlam, the black steer, who gored the enemy; beloved of the god Nebo, who rejoiced the inhabitants of Borsippa, the Sublime; who is indefatigable for E-zida; the divine king of the city; the White, Wise; who broadened the fields of Dilbat, who heaped up the harvests for Urash; the Mighty, the lord to whom come scepter and crown, with which he clothes himself; the Elect of Ma-ma; who fixed the temple bounds of Kesh, who made rich the holy feasts of Nin-tu; the provident, solicitous, who provided food and drink for Lagash and Girsu, who provided large sacrificial offerings for the temple of Ningirsu; who captured the enemy, the Elect of the oracle who fulfilled the prediction of Hallab, who rejoiced the heart of Anunit; the pure prince, whose prayer is accepted by Adad; who satisfied the heart of Adad, the warrior, in Karkar, who restored the vessels for worship in E-ud-gal-gal; the king who granted life to the city of Adab; the guide of E-mach; the princely king of the city, the irresistible warrior, who granted life to the inhabitants of Mashkanshabri, and brought abundance to the temple of Shidlam; the White, Potent, who penetrated the secret cave of the bandits, saved the inhabitants of Malka from misfortune, and fixed their home fast in wealth; who established pure sacrificial gifts for Ea and Dam-gal-nun-na, who made his kingdom everlastingly great; the princely king of the city, who subjected the districts on the Ud-kib-nun-na Canal to the sway of Dagon, his Creator; who spared the inhabitants of Mera and Tutul; the sublime prince, who makes the face of Ninni shine; who presents holy meals to the divinity of Nin-a-zu, who cared for its inhabitants in their need, provided a portion for them in Babylon in peace; the shepherd of the oppressed and of the slaves; whose deeds find favor before Anunit, who provided for Anunit in the temple of Dumash in the suburb of Agade; who recognizes the right, who rules by law; who gave back to the city of Ashur its protecting god; who let the name of Ishtar of Nineveh remain in E-mish-mish; the Sublime, who humbles himself before the great gods; successor of Sumula-il; the mighty son of Sin-muballit; the royal scion of Eternity; the mighty monarch, the sun of Babylon, whose rays shed light over the land of Sumer and Akkad; the king, obeyed by the four quarters of the world; Beloved of Ninni, am I.

When Marduk sent me to rule over men, to give the protection of right to the land, I did right and righteousness in . . . , and brought about the well-being of the oppressed.

CODE OF LAWS

1. If any one ensnare another, putting a ban upon him, but he can not prove it, then he that ensnared him shall be put to death.

2. If any one bring an accusation against a man, and the accused go to the river and leap into the river, if he sink in the river his accuser shall take possession of his house. But if the river prove that the accused is not guilty, and he escape unhurt, then he who had brought the accusation shall be put to death, while he who leaped into the river shall take possession of the house that had belonged to his accuser.

3. If any one bring an accusation of any crime before the elders, and does not prove what he has charged, he shall, if it be a capital offense charged, be put to death.

4. If he satisfy the elders to impose a fine of grain or money, he shall receive the fine that the action produces.

5. If a judge try a case, reach a decision, and present his judgment in writing; if later error shall appear in his decision, and it be through his own fault, then he shall pay twelve times the fine set by him in the case, and he shall be publicly removed from the

judge's bench, and never again shall he sit there to render judgement.

6. If any one steal the property of a temple or of the court, he shall be put to death, and also the one who receives the stolen thing from him shall be put to death.

7. If any one buy from the son or the slave of another man, without witnesses or a contract, silver or gold, a male or female slave, an ox or a sheep, an ass or anything, or if he take it in charge, he is considered a thief and shall be put to death.

8. If any one steal cattle or sheep, or an ass, or a pig or a goat, if it belong to a god or to the court, the thief shall pay thirtyfold therefor; if they belonged to a freed man of the king he shall pay tenfold; if the thief has nothing with which to pay he shall be put to death.

9. If any one lose an article, and find it in the possession of another: if the person in whose possession the thing is found say "A merchant sold it to me, I paid for it before witnesses," and if the owner of the thing say, "I will bring witnesses who know my property," then shall the purchaser bring the merchant who sold it to him, and the witnesses before whom he bought it, and the owner shall bring witnesses who can identify his property. The judge shall examine their testimony--both of the witnesses before whom the price was paid, and of the witnesses who identify the lost article on oath. The merchant is then proved to be a thief and shall be put to death. The owner of the lost article receives his property, and he who bought it receives the money he paid from the estate of the merchant.

10. If the purchaser does not bring the merchant and the witnesses before whom he bought the article, but its owner bring witnesses who identify it, then the buyer is the thief and shall be put to death, and the owner receives the lost article.

11. If the owner do not bring witnesses to identify the lost article, he is an evil-doer, he has traduced, and shall be put to death.

12. If the witnesses be not at hand, then shall the judge set a limit, at the expiration of six months. If his witnesses have not appeared within the six months, he is an evil-doer, and shall bear the fine of the pending case.

[editor's note: there is no 13th law in the code, 13 being considered and unlucky and evil number]

14. If any one steal the minor son of another, he shall be put to death.

15. If any one take a male or female slave of the court, or a male or female slave of a freed man, outside the city gates, he shall be put to death.

16. If any one receive into his house a runaway male or female slave of the court, or of a freedman, and does not bring it out at the public proclamation of the major domus, the master of the house shall be put to death.

17. If any one find runaway male or female slaves in the open country and bring them to their masters, the master of the slaves shall pay him two shekels of silver.

18. If the slave will not give the name of the master, the finder shall bring him to the palace; a further investigation must follow, and the slave shall be returned to his master.

19. If he hold the slaves in his house, and they are caught there, he shall be put to death.

20. If the slave that he caught run away from him, then shall he swear to the owners of the slave, and he is free of all blame.

21. If any one break a hole into a house (break in to steal), he shall be put to death before that hole and be buried.

22. If any one is committing a robbery and is caught, then he shall be put to death.

23. If the robber is not caught, then shall he who was robbed claim under oath the amount of his loss; then shall the community, and . . . on whose ground and territory and in whose domain it was compensate him for the goods stolen.

24. If persons are stolen, then shall the community and . . . pay one mina of silver to their relatives.

25. If fire break out in a house, and some one who comes to put it out cast his eye upon the property of the owner of the house, and take the property of the master of the house, he shall be thrown into that self-same fire.

26. If a chieftain or a man (common soldier), who has been ordered to go upon the king's highway for war does not go, but hires

a mercenary, if he withholds the compensation, then shall this officer or man be put to death, and he who represented him shall take possession of his house.

27. If a chieftain or man be caught in the misfortune of the king (captured in battle), and if his fields and garden be given to another and he take possession, if he return and reaches his place, his field and garden shall be returned to him, he shall take it over again.

28. If a chieftain or a man be caught in the misfortune of a king, if his son is able to enter into possession, then the field and garden shall be given to him, he shall take over the fee of his father.

29. If his son is still young, and can not take possession, a third of the field and garden shall be given to his mother, and she shall bring him up.

30. If a chieftain or a man leave his house, garden, and field and hires it out, and some one else takes possession of his house, garden, and field and uses it for three years: if the first owner return and claims his house, garden, and field, it shall not be given to him, but he who has taken possession of it and used it shall continue to use it.

31. If he hire it out for one year and then return, the house, garden, and field shall be given back to him, and he shall take it over again.

32. If a chieftain or a man is captured on the "Way of the King" (in war), and a merchant buy him free, and bring him back to his place; if he have the means in his house to buy his freedom, he shall buy himself free: if he have nothing in his house with which to buy himself free, he shall be bought free by the temple of his community; if there be nothing in the temple with which to buy him free, the court shall buy his freedom. His field, garden, and house shall not be given for the purchase of his freedom.

33. If a ... or a ... enter himself as withdrawn from the "Way of the King," and send a mercenary as substitute, but withdraw him, then the ... or ... shall be put to death.

34. If a ... or a ... harm the property of a captain, injure the captain, or take away from the captain a gift presented to him by the king, then the ... or ... shall be put to death.

35. If any one buy the cattle or sheep which the king has given to chieftains from him, he loses his money.

36. The field, garden, and house of a chieftain, of a man, or of one subject to quit-rent, can not be sold.

37. If any one buy the field, garden, and house of a chieftain, man, or one subject to quit-rent, his contract tablet of sale shall be broken (declared invalid) and he loses his money. The field, garden, and house return to their owners.

38. A chieftain, man, or one subject to quit-rent can not assign his tenure of field, house, and garden to his wife or daughter, nor can he assign it for a debt.

39. He may, however, assign a field, garden, or house which he has bought, and holds as property, to his wife or daughter or give it for debt.

40. He may sell field, garden, and house to a merchant (royal agents) or to any other public official, the buyer holding field, house, and garden for its usufruct.

41. If any one fence in the field, garden, and house of a chieftain, man, or one subject to quit-rent, furnishing the palings therefor; if the chieftain, man, or one subject to quit-rent return to field, garden, and house, the palings which were given to him become his property.

42. If any one take over a field to till it, and obtain no harvest therefrom, it must be proved that he did no work on the field, and he must deliver grain, just as his neighbor raised, to the owner of the field.

43. If he do not till the field, but let it lie fallow, he shall give grain like his neighbor's to the owner of the field, and the field which he let lie fallow he must plow and sow and return to its owner.

44. If any one take over a waste-lying field to make it arable, but is lazy, and does not make it arable, he shall plow the fallow field in the fourth year, harrow it and till it, and give it back to its owner, and for each ten gan (a measure of area) ten gur of grain shall be paid.

45. If a man rent his field for tillage for a fixed rental, and receive the rent of his field, but bad weather come and destroy the harvest, the injury falls upon the tiller of the soil.

46. If he do not receive a fixed rental for his field, but lets it on half or third shares of the harvest, the grain on the field shall be divided proportionately between the tiller and the owner.

47. If the tiller, because he did not succeed in the first year, has had the soil tilled by others, the owner may raise no objection; the field has been cultivated and he receives the harvest according to agreement.

48. If any one owe a debt for a loan, and a storm prostrates the grain, or the harvest fail, or the grain does not grow for lack of water; in that year he need not give his creditor any grain, he washes his debt-tablet in water and pays no rent for this year.

49. If any one take money from a merchant, and give the merchant a field tillable for corn or sesame and order him to plant corn or sesame in the field, and to harvest the crop; if the cultivator plant corn or sesame in the field, at the harvest the corn or sesame that is in the field shall belong to the owner of the field and he shall pay corn as rent, for the money he received from the merchant, and the livelihood of the cultivator shall he give to the merchant.

50. If he give a cultivated corn-field or a cultivated sesame-field, the corn or sesame in the field shall belong to the owner of the field, and he shall return the money to the merchant as rent.

51. If he have no money to repay, then he shall pay in corn or sesame in place of the money as rent for what he received from the merchant, according to the royal tariff.

52. If the cultivator do not plant corn or sesame in the field, the debtor's contract is not weakened.

53. If any one be too lazy to keep his dam in proper condition, and does not so keep it; if then the dam break and all the fields be flooded, then shall he in whose dam the break occurred be sold for money, and the money shall replace the corn which he has caused to be ruined.

54. If he be not able to replace the corn, then he and his possessions shall be divided among the farmers whose corn he has flooded.

55. If any one open his ditches to water his crop, but is careless, and the water flood the field of his neighbor, then he shall pay his neighbor corn for his loss.

56. If a man let in the water, and the water overflow the plantation of his neighbor, he shall pay ten gur of corn for every ten gan of land.

57. If a shepherd, without the permission of the owner of the

field, and without the knowledge of the owner of the sheep, lets the sheep into a field to graze, then the owner of the field shall harvest his crop, and the shepherd, who had pastured his flock there without permission of the owner of the field, shall pay to the owner twenty gur of corn for every ten gan.

58. If after the flocks have left the pasture and been shut up in the common fold at the city gate, any shepherd let them into a field and they graze there, this shepherd shall take possession of the field which he has allowed to be grazed on, and at the harvest he must pay sixty gur of corn for every ten gan.

59. If any man, without the knowledge of the owner of a garden, fell a tree in a garden he shall pay half a mina in money.

60. If any one give over a field to a gardener, for him to plant it as a garden, if he work at it, and care for it for four years, in the fifth year the owner and the gardener shall divide it, the owner taking his part in charge.

61. If the gardener has not completed the planting of the field, leaving one part unused, this shall be assigned to him as his.

62. If he do not plant the field that was given over to him as a garden, if it be arable land (for corn or sesame) the gardener shall pay the owner the produce of the field for the years that he let it lie fallow, according to the product of neighboring fields, put the field in arable condition and return it to its owner.

63. If he transform waste land into arable fields and return it to its owner, the latter shall pay him for one year ten gur for ten gan.

64. If any one hand over his garden to a gardener to work, the gardener shall pay to its owner two-thirds of the produce of the garden, for so long as he has it in possession, and the other third shall he keep.

65. If the gardener do not work in the garden and the product fall off, the gardener shall pay in proportion to other neighboring gardens.

[Here a portion of the text is missing, apparently comprising thirty-four paragraphs.]

100. . . . interest for the money, as much as he has received, he shall give a note therefor, and on the day, when they settle, pay to the merchant.

101. If there are no mercantile arrangements in the place whither he went, he shall leave the entire amount of money which he received with the broker to give to the merchant.

102. If a merchant entrust money to an agent (broker) for some investment, and the broker suffer a loss in the place to which he goes, he shall make good the capital to the merchant.

103. If, while on the journey, an enemy take away from him anything that he had, the broker shall swear by God and be free of obligation.

104. If a merchant give an agent corn, wool, oil, or any other goods to transport, the agent shall give a receipt for the amount, and compensate the merchant therefor. Then he shall obtain a receipt form the merchant for the money that he gives the merchant.

105. If the agent is careless, and does not take a receipt for the money which he gave the merchant, he can not consider the unreceipted money as his own.

106. If the agent accept money from the merchant, but have a quarrel with the merchant (denying the receipt), then shall the merchant swear before God and witnesses that he has given this money to the agent, and the agent shall pay him three times the sum.

107. If the merchant cheat the agent, in that as the latter has returned to him all that had been given him, but the merchant denies the receipt of what had been returned to him, then shall this agent convict the merchant before God and the judges, and if he still deny receiving what the agent had given him shall pay six times the sum to the agent.

108. If a tavern-keeper (feminine) does not accept corn according to gross weight in payment of drink, but takes money, and the price of the drink is less than that of the corn, she shall be convicted and thrown into the water.

109. If conspirators meet in the house of a tavern-keeper, and these conspirators are not captured and delivered to the court, the tavern-keeper shall be put to death.

110. If a "sister of a god" open a tavern, or enter a tavern to drink, then shall this woman be burned to death.

111. If an inn-keeper furnish sixty ka of usakani-drink to . . . she shall receive fifty ka of corn at the harvest.

112. If any one be on a journey and entrust silver, gold, precious stones, or any movable property to another, and wish to recover it from him; if the latter do not bring all of the property to the appointed place, but appropriate it to his own use, then shall this man, who did not bring the property to hand it over, be convicted, and he shall pay fivefold for all that had been entrusted to him.

113. If any one have consignment of corn or money, and he take from the granary or box without the knowledge of the owner, then shall he who took corn without the knowledge of the owner out of the granary or money out of the box be legally convicted, and repay the corn he has taken. And he shall lose whatever commission was paid to him, or due him.

114. If a man have no claim on another for corn and money, and try to demand it by force, he shall pay one-third of a mina of silver in every case.

115. If any one have a claim for corn or money upon another and imprison him; if the prisoner die in prison a natural death, the case shall go no further.

116. If the prisoner die in prison from blows or maltreatment, the master of the prisoner shall convict the merchant before the judge. If he was a free-born man, the son of the merchant shall be put to death; if it was a slave, he shall pay one-third of a mina of gold, and all that the master of the prisoner gave he shall forfeit.

117. If any one fail to meet a claim for debt, and sell himself, his wife, his son, and daughter for money or give them away to forced labor: they shall work for three years in the house of the man who bought them, or the proprietor, and in the fourth year they shall be set free.

118. If he give a male or female slave away for forced labor, and the merchant sublease them, or sell them for money, no objection can be raised.

119. If any one fail to meet a claim for debt, and he sell the maid servant who has borne him children, for money, the money which the merchant has paid shall be repaid to him by the owner of the slave and she shall be freed.

120. If any one store corn for safe keeping in another person's house, and any harm happen to the corn in storage, or if the owner of the house open the granary and take some of the corn, or if especially he deny that the corn was stored in his house: then the owner of the corn shall claim his corn before God (on oath), and the owner of the house shall pay its owner for all of the corn that he took.

121. If any one store corn in another man's house he shall pay him storage at the rate of one gur for every five ka of corn per year.

122. If any one give another silver, gold, or anything else to keep, he shall show everything to some witness, draw up a contract, and then hand it over for safe keeping.

123. If he turn it over for safe keeping without witness or contract, and if he to whom it was given deny it, then he has no legitimate claim.

124. If any one deliver silver, gold, or anything else to another for safe keeping, before a witness, but he deny it, he shall be brought before a judge, and all that he has denied he shall pay in full.

125. If any one place his property with another for safe keeping, and there, either through thieves or robbers, his property and the property of the other man be lost, the owner of the house, through whose neglect the loss took place, shall compensate the owner for all that was given to him in charge. But the owner of the house shall try to follow up and recover his property, and take it away from the thief.

126. If any one who has not lost his goods state that they have been lost, and make false claims: if he claim his goods and amount of injury before God, even though he has not lost them, he shall be fully compensated for all his loss claimed. (I.e., the oath is all that is needed.)

127. If any one "point the finger" (slander) at a sister of a god or the wife of any one, and can not prove it, this man shall be taken before the judges and his brow shall be marked. (by cutting the skin, or perhaps hair.)

128. If a man take a woman to wife, but have no intercourse with her, this woman is no wife to him.

129. If a man's wife be surprised (in flagrante delicto) with

another man, both shall be tied and thrown into the water, but the husband may pardon his wife and the king his slaves.

130. If a man violate the wife (betrothed or child-wife) of another man, who has never known a man, and still lives in her father's house, and sleep with her and be surprised, this man shall be put to death, but the wife is blameless.

131. If a man bring a charge against one's wife, but she is not surprised with another man, she must take an oath and then may return to her house.

132. If the "finger is pointed" at a man's wife about another man, but she is not caught sleeping with the other man, she shall jump into the river for her husband.

133. If a man is taken prisoner in war, and there is a sustenance in his house, but his wife leave house and court, and go to another house: because this wife did not keep her court, and went to another house, she shall be judicially condemned and thrown into the water.

134. If any one be captured in war and there is not sustenance in his house, if then his wife go to another house this woman shall be held blameless.

135. If a man be taken prisoner in war and there be no sustenance in his house and his wife go to another house and bear children; and if later her husband return and come to his home: then this wife shall return to her husband, but the children follow their father.

136. If any one leave his house, run away, and then his wife go to another house, if then he return, and wishes to take his wife back: because he fled from his home and ran away, the wife of this runaway shall not return to her husband.

137. If a man wish to separate from a woman who has borne him children, or from his wife who has borne him children: then he shall give that wife her dowry, and a part of the usufruct of field, garden, and property, so that she can rear her children. When she has brought up her children, a portion of all that is given to the children, equal as that of one son, shall be given to her. She may then marry the man of her heart.

138. If a man wishes to separate from his wife who has borne him no children, he shall give her the amount of her purchase money and the dowry which she brought from her father's house, and let her go.

139. If there was no purchase price he shall give her one mina of gold as a gift of release.

140. If he be a freed man he shall give her one-third of a mina of gold.

141. If a man's wife, who lives in his house, wishes to leave it, plunges into debt, tries to ruin her house, neglects her husband, and is judicially convicted: if her husband offer her release, she may go on her way, and he gives her nothing as a gift of release. If her husband does not wish to release her, and if he take another wife, she shall remain as servant in her husband's house.

142. If a woman quarrel with her husband, and say: "You are not congenial to me," the reasons for her prejudice must be presented. If she is guiltless, and there is no fault on her part, but he leaves and neglects her, then no guilt attaches to this woman, she shall take her dowry and go back to her father's house.

143. If she is not innocent, but leaves her husband, and ruins her house, neglecting her husband, this woman shall be cast into the water.

144. If a man take a wife and this woman give her husband a maid-servant, and she bear him children, but this man wishes to take another wife, this shall not be permitted to him; he shall not take a second wife.

145. If a man take a wife, and she bear him no children, and he intend to take another wife: if he take this second wife, and bring her into the house, this second wife shall not be allowed equality with his wife.

146. If a man take a wife and she give this man a maid-servant as wife and she bear him children, and then this maid assume equality with the wife: because she has borne him children her master shall not sell her for money, but he may keep her as a slave, reckoning her among the maid-servants.

147. If she have not borne him children, then her mistress may sell her for money.

148. If a man take a wife, and she be seized by disease, if he then desire to take a second wife he shall not put away his wife, who has been attacked by disease, but he shall keep her in the house which he has built and support her so long as she lives.

149. If this woman does not wish to remain in her husband's house, then he shall compensate her for the dowry that she brought with her from her father's house, and she may go.

150. If a man give his wife a field, garden, and house and a deed therefor, if then after the death of her husband the sons raise no claim, then the mother may bequeath all to one of her sons whom she prefers, and need leave nothing to his brothers.

151. If a woman who lived in a man's house made an agreement with her husband, that no creditor can arrest her, and has given a document therefor: if that man, before he married that woman, had a debt, the creditor can not hold the woman for it. But if the woman, before she entered the man's house, had contracted a debt, her creditor can not arrest her husband therefor.

152. If after the woman had entered the man's house, both contracted a debt, both must pay the merchant.

153. If the wife of one man on account of another man has their mates (her husband and the other man's wife) murdered, both of them shall be impaled.

154. If a man be guilty of incest with his daughter, he shall be driven from the place (exiled).

155. If a man betroth a girl to his son, and his son have intercourse with her, but he (the father) afterward defile her, and be surprised, then he shall be bound and cast into the water (drowned).

156. If a man betroth a girl to his son, but his son has not known her, and if then he defile her, he shall pay her half a gold mina, and compensate her for all that she brought out of her father's house. She may marry the man of her heart.

157. If any one be guilty of incest with his mother after his father, both shall be burned.

158. If any one be surprised after his father with his chief wife, who has borne children, he shall be driven out of his father's house.

159. If any one, who has brought chattels into his father-in-law's house, and has paid the purchase-money, looks for another wife, and says to his father-in-law: "I do not want your daughter," the girl's father may keep all that he had brought.

160. If a man bring chattels into the house of his father-in-law, and pay the "purchase price" (for his wife): if then the father of the

girl say: "I will not give you my daughter," he shall give him back all that he brought with him.

161. If a man bring chattels into his father-in-law's house and pay the "purchase price," if then his friend slander him, and his father-in-law say to the young husband: "You shall not marry my daughter," the he shall give back to him undiminished all that he had brought with him; but his wife shall not be married to the friend.

162. If a man marry a woman, and she bear sons to him; if then this woman die, then shall her father have no claim on her dowry; this belongs to her sons.

163. If a man marry a woman and she bear him no sons; if then this woman die, if the "purchase price" which he had paid into the house of his father-in-law is repaid to him, her husband shall have no claim upon the dowry of this woman; it belongs to her father's house.

164. If his father-in-law do not pay back to him the amount of the "purchase price" he may subtract the amount of the "Purchase price" from the dowry, and then pay the remainder to her father's house.

165. If a man give to one of his sons whom he prefers a field, garden, and house, and a deed therefor: if later the father die, and the brothers divide the estate, then they shall first give him the present of his father, and he shall accept it; and the rest of the paternal property shall they divide.

166. If a man take wives for his son, but take no wife for his minor son, and if then he die: if the sons divide the estate, they shall set aside besides his portion the money for the "purchase price" for the minor brother who had taken no wife as yet, and secure a wife for him.

167. If a man marry a wife and she bear him children: if this wife die and he then take another wife and she bear him children: if then the father die, the sons must not partition the estate according to the mothers, they shall divide the dowries of their mothers only in this way; the paternal estate they shall divide equally with one another.

168. If a man wish to put his son out of his house, and declare before the judge: "I want to put my son out," then the judge shall

examine into his reasons. If the son be guilty of no great fault, for which he can be rightfully put out, the father shall not put him out.

169. If he be guilty of a grave fault, which should rightfully deprive him of the filial relationship, the father shall forgive him the first time; but if he be guilty of a grave fault a second time the father may deprive his son of all filial relation.

170. If his wife bear sons to a man, or his maid-servant have borne sons, and the father while still living says to the children whom his maid-servant has borne: "My sons," and he count them with the sons of his wife; if then the father die, then the sons of the wife and of the maid-servant shall divide the paternal property in common. The son of the wife is to partition and choose.

171. If, however, the father while still living did not say to the sons of the maid-servant: "My sons," and then the father dies, then the sons of the maid-servant shall not share with the sons of the wife, but the freedom of the maid and her sons shall be granted. The sons of the wife shall have no right to enslave the sons of the maid; the wife shall take her dowry (from her father), and the gift that her husband gave her and deeded to her (separate from dowry, or the purchase-money paid her father), and live in the home of her husband: so long as she lives she shall use it, it shall not be sold for money. Whatever she leaves shall belong to her children.

172. If her husband made her no gift, she shall be compensated for her gift, and she shall receive a portion from the estate of her husband, equal to that of one child. If her sons oppress her, to force her out of the house, the judge shall examine into the matter, and if the sons are at fault the woman shall not leave her husband's house. If the woman desire to leave the house, she must leave to her sons the gift which her husband gave her, but she may take the dowry of her father's house. Then she may marry the man of her heart.

173. If this woman bear sons to her second husband, in the place to which she went, and then die, her earlier and later sons shall divide the dowry between them.

174. If she bear no sons to her second husband, the sons of her first husband shall have the dowry.

175. If a State slave or the slave of a freed man marry the daughter

of a free man, and children are born, the master of the slave shall have no right to enslave the children of the free.

176. If, however, a State slave or the slave of a freed man marry a man's daughter, and after he marries her she bring a dowry from a father's house, if then they both enjoy it and found a household, and accumulate means, if then the slave die, then she who was free born may take her dowry, and all that her husband and she had earned; she shall divide them into two parts, one-half the master for the slave shall take, and the other half shall the free-born woman take for her children. If the free-born woman had no gift she shall take all that her husband and she had earned and divide it into two parts; and the master of the slave shall take one-half and she shall take the other for her children.

177. If a widow, whose children are not grown, wishes to enter another house (remarry), she shall not enter it without the knowledge of the judge. If she enter another house the judge shall examine the state of the house of her first husband. Then the house of her first husband shall be entrusted to the second husband and the woman herself as managers. And a record must be made thereof. She shall keep the house in order, bring up the children, and not sell the house-hold utensils. He who buys the utensils of the children of a widow shall lose his money, and the goods shall return to their owners.

178. If a "devoted woman" or a prostitute to whom her father has given a dowry and a deed therefor, but if in this deed it is not stated that she may bequeath it as she pleases, and has not explicitly stated that she has the right of disposal; if then her father die, then her brothers shall hold her field and garden, and give her corn, oil, and milk according to her portion, and satisfy her. If her brothers do not give her corn, oil, and milk according to her share, then her field and garden shall support her. She shall have the usufruct of field and garden and all that her father gave her so long as she lives, but she can not sell or assign it to others. Her position of inheritance belongs to her brothers.

179. If a "sister of a god," or a prostitute, receive a gift from her father, and a deed in which it has been explicitly stated that she may dispose of it as she pleases, and give her complete disposition

thereof: if then her father die, then she may leave her property to whomsoever she pleases. Her brothers can raise no claim thereto.

180. If a father give a present to his daughter--either marriageable or a prostitute (unmarriageable)--and then die, then she is to receive a portion as a child from the paternal estate, and enjoy its usufruct so long as she lives. Her estate belongs to her brothers.

181. If a father devote a temple-maid or temple-virgin to God and give her no present: if then the father die, she shall receive the third of a child's portion from the inheritance of her father's house, and enjoy its usufruct so long as she lives. Her estate belongs to her brothers.

182. If a father devote his daughter as a wife of Mardi of Babylon (as in 181), and give her no present, nor a deed; if then her father die, then shall she receive one-third of her portion as a child of her father's house from her brothers, but Marduk may leave her estate to whomsoever she wishes.

183. If a man give his daughter by a concubine a dowry, and a husband, and a deed; if then her father die, she shall receive no portion from the paternal estate.

184. If a man do not give a dowry to his daughter by a concubine, and no husband; if then her father die, her brother shall give her a dowry according to her father's wealth and secure a husband for her.

185. If a man adopt a child and to his name as son, and rear him, this grown son can not be demanded back again.

186. If a man adopt a son, and if after he has taken him he injure his foster father and mother, then this adopted son shall return to his father's house.

187. The son of a paramour in the palace service, or of a prostitute, can not be demanded back.

188. If an artizan has undertaken to rear a child and teaches him his craft, he can not be demanded back.

189. If he has not taught him his craft, this adopted son may return to his father's house.

190. If a man does not maintain a child that he has adopted as a son and reared with his other children, then his adopted son may return to his father's house.

191. If a man, who had adopted a son and reared him, founded a

household, and had children, wish to put this adopted son out, then this son shall not simply go his way. His adoptive father shall give him of his wealth one-third of a child's portion, and then he may go. He shall not give him of the field, garden, and house.

192. If a son of a paramour or a prostitute say to his adoptive father or mother: "You are not my father, or my mother," his tongue shall be cut off.

193. If the son of a paramour or a prostitute desire his father's house, and desert his adoptive father and adoptive mother, and goes to his father's house, then shall his eye be put out.

194. If a man give his child to a nurse and the child die in her hands, but the nurse unbeknown to the father and mother nurse another child, then they shall convict her of having nursed another child without the knowledge of the father and mother and her breasts shall be cut off.

195. If a son strike his father, his hands shall be hewn off.

196. If a man put out the eye of another man, his eye shall be put out. [An eye for an eye]

197. If he break another man's bone, his bone shall be broken.

198. If he put out the eye of a freed man, or break the bone of a freed man, he shall pay one gold mina.

199. If he put out the eye of a man's slave, or break the bone of a man's slave, he shall pay one-half of its value.

200. If a man knock out the teeth of his equal, his teeth shall be knocked out. [A tooth for a tooth]

201. If he knock out the teeth of a freed man, he shall pay one-third of a gold mina.

202. If any one strike the body of a man higher in rank than he, he shall receive sixty blows with an ox-whip in public.

203. If a free-born man strike the body of another free-born man or equal rank, he shall pay one gold mina.

204. If a freed man strike the body of another freed man, he shall pay ten shekels in money.

205. If the slave of a freed man strike the body of a freed man, his ear shall be cut off.

206. If during a quarrel one man strike another and wound him,

then he shall swear, "I did not injure him wittingly," and pay the physicians.

207. If the man die of his wound, he shall swear similarly, and if he (the deceased) was a free-born man, he shall pay half a mina in money.

208. If he was a freed man, he shall pay one-third of a mina.

209. If a man strike a free-born woman so that she lose her unborn child, he shall pay ten shekels for her loss.

210. If the woman die, his daughter shall be put to death.

211. If a woman of the free class lose her child by a blow, he shall pay five shekels in money.

212. If this woman die, he shall pay half a mina.

213. If he strike the maid-servant of a man, and she lose her child, he shall pay two shekels in money.

214. If this maid-servant die, he shall pay one-third of a mina.

215. If a physician make a large incision with an operating knife and cure it, or if he open a tumor (over the eye) with an operating knife, and saves the eye, he shall receive ten shekels in money.

216. If the patient be a freed man, he receives five shekels.

217. If he be the slave of some one, his owner shall give the physician two shekels.

218. If a physician make a large incision with the operating knife, and kill him, or open a tumor with the operating knife, and cut out the eye, his hands shall be cut off.

219. If a physician make a large incision in the slave of a freed man, and kill him, he shall replace the slave with another slave.

220. If he had opened a tumor with the operating knife, and put out his eye, he shall pay half his value.

221. If a physician heal the broken bone or diseased soft part of a man, the patient shall pay the physician five shekels in money.

222. If he were a freed man he shall pay three shekels.

223. If he were a slave his owner shall pay the physician two shekels.

224. If a veterinary surgeon perform a serious operation on an ass or an ox, and cure it, the owner shall pay the surgeon one-sixth of a shekel as a fee.

225. If he perform a serious operation on an ass or ox, and kill it, he shall pay the owner one-fourth of its value.

226. If a barber, without the knowledge of his master, cut the sign of a slave on a slave not to be sold, the hands of this barber shall be cut off.

227. If any one deceive a barber, and have him mark a slave not for sale with the sign of a slave, he shall be put to death, and buried in his house. The barber shall swear: "I did not mark him wittingly," and shall be guiltless.

228. If a builder build a house for some one and complete it, he shall give him a fee of two shekels in money for each sar of surface.

229 If a builder build a house for some one, and does not construct it properly, and the house which he built fall in and kill its owner, then that builder shall be put to death.

230. If it kill the son of the owner the son of that builder shall be put to death.

231. If it kill a slave of the owner, then he shall pay slave for slave to the owner of the house.

232. If it ruin goods, he shall make compensation for all that has been ruined, and inasmuch as he did not construct properly this house which he built and it fell, he shall re-erect the house from his own means.

233. If a builder build a house for some one, even though he has not yet completed it; if then the walls seem toppling, the builder must make the walls solid from his own means.

234. If a shipbuilder build a boat of sixty gur for a man, he shall pay him a fee of two shekels in money.

235. If a shipbuilder build a boat for some one, and do not make it tight, if during that same year that boat is sent away and suffers injury, the shipbuilder shall take the boat apart and put it together tight at his own expense. The tight boat he shall give to the boat owner.

236. If a man rent his boat to a sailor, and the sailor is careless, and the boat is wrecked or goes aground, the sailor shall give the owner of the boat another boat as compensation.

237. If a man hire a sailor and his boat, and provide it with corn, clothing, oil and dates, and other things of the kind needed for fitting

it: if the sailor is careless, the boat is wrecked, and its contents ruined, then the sailor shall compensate for the boat which was wrecked and all in it that he ruined.

238. If a sailor wreck any one's ship, but saves it, he shall pay the half of its value in money.

239. If a man hire a sailor, he shall pay him six gur of corn per year.

240. If a merchantman run against a ferryboat, and wreck it, the master of the ship that was wrecked shall seek justice before God; the master of the merchantman, which wrecked the ferryboat, must compensate the owner for the boat and all that he ruined.

241. If any one impresses an ox for forced labor, he shall pay one-third of a mina in money.

242. If any one hire oxen for a year, he shall pay four gur of corn for plow-oxen.

243. As rent of herd cattle he shall pay three gur of corn to the owner.

244. If any one hire an ox or an ass, and a lion kill it in the field, the loss is upon its owner.

245. If any one hire oxen, and kill them by bad treatment or blows, he shall compensate the owner, oxen for oxen.

246. If a man hire an ox, and he break its leg or cut the ligament of its neck, he shall compensate the owner with ox for ox.

247. If any one hire an ox, and put out its eye, he shall pay the owner one-half of its value.

248. If any one hire an ox, and break off a horn, or cut off its tail, or hurt its muzzle, he shall pay one-fourth of its value in money.

249. If any one hire an ox, and God strike it that it die, the man who hired it shall swear by God and be considered guiltless.

250. If while an ox is passing on the street (market) some one push it, and kill it, the owner can set up no claim in the suit (against the hirer).

251. If an ox be a goring ox, and it shown that he is a gorer, and he do not bind his horns, or fasten the ox up, and the ox gore a free-born man and kill him, the owner shall pay one-half a mina in money.

252. If he kill a man's slave, he shall pay one-third of a mina.

253. If any one agree with another to tend his field, give him seed,

entrust a yoke of oxen to him, and bind him to cultivate the field, if he steal the corn or plants, and take them for himself, his hands shall be hewn off.

254. If he take the seed-corn for himself, and do not use the yoke of oxen, he shall compensate him for the amount of the seed-corn.

255. If he sublet the man's yoke of oxen or steal the seed-corn, planting nothing in the field, he shall be convicted, and for each one hundred gan he shall pay sixty gur of corn.

256. If his community will not pay for him, then he shall be placed in that field with the cattle (at work).

257. If any one hire a field laborer, he shall pay him eight gur of corn per year.

258. If any one hire an ox-driver, he shall pay him six gur of corn per year.

259. If any one steal a water-wheel from the field, he shall pay five shekels in money to its owner.

260. If any one steal a shadduf (used to draw water from the river or canal) or a plow, he shall pay three shekels in money.

261. If any one hire a herdsman for cattle or sheep, he shall pay him eight gur of corn per annum.

262. If any one, a cow or a sheep . . .

263. If he kill the cattle or sheep that were given to him, he shall compensate the owner with cattle for cattle and sheep for sheep.

264. If a herdsman, to whom cattle or sheep have been entrusted for watching over, and who has received his wages as agreed upon, and is satisfied, diminish the number of the cattle or sheep, or make the increase by birth less, he shall make good the increase or profit which was lost in the terms of settlement.

265. If a herdsman, to whose care cattle or sheep have been entrusted, be guilty of fraud and make false returns of the natural increase, or sell them for money, then shall he be convicted and pay the owner ten times the loss.

266. If the animal be killed in the stable by God (an accident), or if a lion kill it, the herdsman shall declare his innocence before God, and the owner bears the accident in the stable.

267. If the herdsman overlook something, and an accident happen in the stable, then the herdsman is at fault for the accident

which he has caused in the stable, and he must compensate the owner for the cattle or sheep.

268. If any one hire an ox for threshing, the amount of the hire is twenty ka of corn.

269. If he hire an ass for threshing, the hire is twenty ka of corn.

270. If he hire a young animal for threshing, the hire is ten ka of corn.

271. If any one hire oxen, cart and driver, he shall pay one hundred and eighty ka of corn per day.

272. If any one hire a cart alone, he shall pay forty ka of corn per day.

273. If any one hire a day laborer, he shall pay him from the New Year until the fifth month (April to August, when days are long and the work hard) six gerahs in money per day; from the sixth month to the end of the year he shall give him five gerahs per day.

274. If any one hire a skilled artizan, he shall pay as wages of the . . . five gerahs, as wages of the potter five gerahs, of a tailor five gerahs, of . . . gerahs, . . . of a ropemaker four gerahs, of . . . .. gerahs, of a mason . . . gerahs per day.

275. If any one hire a ferryboat, he shall pay three gerahs in money per day.

276. If he hire a freight-boat, he shall pay two and one-half gerahs per day.

277. If any one hire a ship of sixty gur, he shall pay one-sixth of a shekel in money as its hire per day.

278. If any one buy a male or female slave, and before a month has elapsed the benu-disease be developed, he shall return the slave to the seller, and receive the money which he had paid.

279. If any one by a male or female slave, and a third party claim it, the seller is liable for the claim.

280. If while in a foreign country a man buy a male or female slave belonging to another of his own country; if when he return home the owner of the male or female slave recognize it: if the male or female slave be a native of the country, he shall give them back without any money.

281. If they are from another country, the buyer shall declare the

amount of money paid therefor to the merchant, and keep the male or female slave.

282. If a slave say to his master: "You are not my master," if they convict him his master shall cut off his ear.

Epilogue

LAWS of justice which Hammurabi, the wise king, established. A righteous law, and pious statute did he teach the land. Hammurabi, the protecting king am I. I have not withdrawn myself from the men, whom Bel gave to me, the rule over whom Marduk gave to me, I was not negligent, but I made them a peaceful abiding-place. I expounded all great difficulties, I made the light shine upon them. With the mighty weapons which Zamama and Ishtar entrusted to me, with the keen vision with which Ea endowed me, with the wisdom that Marduk gave me, I have uprooted the enemy above and below (in north and south), subdued the earth, brought prosperity to the land, guaranteed security to the inhabitants in their homes; a disturber was not permitted. The great gods have called me, I am the salvation-bearing shepherd, whose staff is straight, the good shadow that is spread over my city; on my breast I cherish the inhabitants of the land of Sumer and Akkad; in my shelter I have let them repose in peace; in my deep wisdom have I enclosed them. That the strong might not injure the weak, in order to protect the widows and orphans, I have in Babylon the city where Anu and Bel raise high their head, in E-Sagil, the Temple, whose foundations stand firm as heaven and earth, in order to bespeak justice in the land, to settle all disputes, and heal all injuries, set up these my precious words, written upon my memorial stone, before the image of me, as king of righteousness.

The king who ruleth among the kings of the cities am I. My words are well considered; there is no wisdom like unto mine. By the command of Shamash, the great judge of heaven and earth, let righteousness go forth in the land: by the order of Marduk, my lord, let no destruction befall my monument. In E-Sagil, which I love, let my name be ever repeated; let the oppressed, who has a case at law, come and stand before this my image as king of righteousness; let him read the inscription, and understand my precious words: the inscription will explain his case to him; he will find out what is just, and his heart will be glad, so that he will say:

"Hammurabi is a ruler, who is as a father to his subjects, who holds the words of Marduk in reverence, who has achieved conquest for Marduk over the north and south, who rejoices the heart of Marduk, his lord, who has bestowed benefits for ever and ever on his subjects, and has established order in the land."

When he reads the record, let him pray with full heart to Marduk, my lord, and Zarpanit, my lady; and then shall the protecting deities and the gods, who frequent E-Sagil, graciously grant the desires daily presented before Marduk, my lord, and Zarpanit, my lady. In future time, through all coming generations, let the king, who may be in the land, observe the words of righteousness which I have written on my monument; let him not alter the law of the land which I have given, the edicts which I have enacted; my monument let him not mar. If such a ruler have wisdom, and be able to keep his land in order, he shall observe the words which I have written in this inscription; the rule, statute, and law of the land which I have given; the decisions which I have made will this inscription show him; let him rule his subjects accordingly, speak justice to them, give right decisions, root out the miscreants and criminals from this land, and grant prosperity to his subjects.

Hammurabi, the king of righteousness, on whom Shamash has conferred right (or law) am I. My words are well considered; my deeds are not equaled; to bring low those that were high; to humble the proud, to expel insolence. If a succeeding ruler considers my words, which I have written in this my inscription, if he do not annul my law, nor corrupt my words, nor change my monument, then may Shamash lengthen that king's reign, as he has that of me, the king of righteousness, that he may reign in righteousness over his subjects. If this ruler do not esteem my words, which I have written in my inscription, if he despise my curses, and fear not the curse of God, if he destroy the law which I have given, corrupt my words, change my monument, efface my name, write his name there, or on account of the curses commission another so to do, that man, whether king or ruler, patesi, or commoner, no matter what he be, may the great God

(Anu), the Father of the gods, who has ordered my rule, withdraw from him the glory of royalty, break his scepter, curse his destiny. May Bel, the lord, who fixeth destiny, whose command can not be altered, who has made my kingdom great, order a rebellion which his hand can not control; may he let the wind of the overthrow of his habitation blow, may he ordain the years of his rule in groaning, years of scarcity, years of famine, darkness without light, death with seeing eyes be fated to him; may he (Bel) order with his potent mouth the destruction of his city, the dispersion of his subjects, the cutting off of his rule, the removal of his name and memory from the land. May Belit, the great Mother, whose command is potent in E-Kur (the Babylonian Olympus), the Mistress, who harkens graciously to my petitions, in the seat of judgment and decision (where Bel fixes destiny), turn his affairs evil before Bel, and put the devastation of his land, the destruction of his subjects, the pouring out of his life like water into the mouth of King Bel. May Ea, the great ruler, whose fated decrees come to pass, the thinker of the gods, the omniscient, who maketh long the days of my life, withdraw understanding and wisdom from him, lead him to forgetfulness, shut up his rivers at their sources, and not allow corn or sustenance for man to grow in his land. May Shamash, the great Judge of heaven and earth, who supporteth all means of livelihood, Lord of life-courage, shatter his dominion, annul his law, destroy his way, make vain the march of his troops, send him in his visions forecasts of the uprooting of the foundations of his throne and of the destruction of his land. May the condemnation of Shamash overtake him forthwith; may he be deprived of water above among the living, and his spirit below in the earth. May Sin (the Moon-god), the Lord of Heaven, the divine father, whose crescent gives light among the gods, take away the crown and regal throne from him; may he put upon him heavy guilt, great decay, that nothing may be lower than he. May he destine him as fated, days, months and years of dominion filled with sighing and tears, increase of the burden of dominion, a life that is like unto death. May Adad, the lord of fruitfulness, ruler of heaven and earth, my helper, withhold from him rain from heaven, and the flood of water from the springs, destroying his land by famine and want; may he rage mightily over his city, and make his land into flood-hills (heaps of ruined cities). May Zamama, the great warrior, the first-born son of E-Kur, who goeth at my right hand, shatter his weapons on the field of battle, turn day into night for him, and let his foe triumph over him. May Ishtar, the goddess of fighting and war, who unfetters my weapons, my gracious protecting spirit, who loveth my dominion, curse his kingdom in her angry heart; in her great wrath, change his grace into evil, and shatter his weapons on the place of fighting and war. May she create disorder and sedition for him, strike down his warriors, that the earth may drink their blood, and throw down the piles of corpses of his warriors on the field; may she not grant him a life of mercy, deliver him into the hands of his enemies, and imprison him in the land of his enemies. May Nergal, the might among the gods, whose contest is irresistible, who grants me victory, in his great might burn up his subjects like a slender reedstalk, cut off his limbs with his mighty weapons, and shatter him like an earthen image. May Nin-tu, the sublime mistress of the lands, the fruitful mother, deny him a son, vouchsafe him no name, give him no successor among men. May Nin-karak, the daughter of Anu, who adjudges grace to me, cause to come upon his members in E-kur high fever, severe wounds, that can not be healed, whose nature the physician does not understand, which he can not treat with dressing, which, like the bite of death, can not be removed, until they have sapped away his life.

May he lament the loss of his life-power, and may the great gods of heaven and earth, the Anunaki, altogether inflict a curse and evil upon the confines of the temple, the walls of this E-barra (the Sun temple of Sippara), upon his dominion, his land, his warriors, his subjects, and his troops. May Bel curse him with the potent curses of his mouth that can not be altered, and may they come upon him forthwith.

PART TWO
TRANSLATION BY ROBERT FRANCIS HARPER

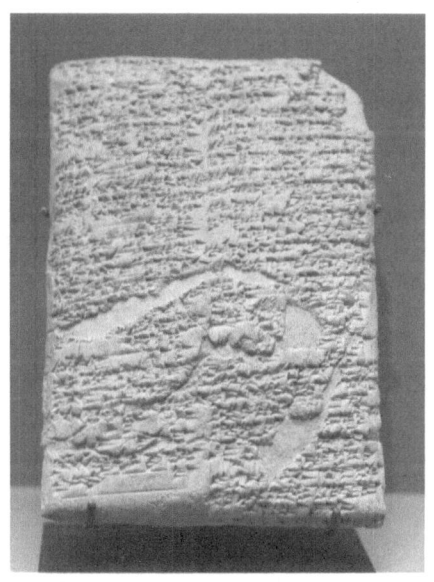

Prologue of the Code of Hammurabi (the 305 first inscripted squares on the stele). Some gaps in the list of benefits bestowed on cities recently annexed by Hammurabi may prove the tablet is older than the celebrated basalt stele (also in the Louvre).

HAMMURABI'S CODE OF LAWS

Prologue

When the lofty Anu, king of the Anunnaki, and Bel, lord of heaven and earth, he who determines the destiny of the land, committed the rule of all mankind to Marduk, the chief son of Ea; when they made him great among the Igigi; when they pronounced the lofty name of Babylon; when they made it famous among the quarters of the world and in its midst established an everlasting kingdom whose foundations were firm as heaven and earth —at that time, Anu and Bel called me, Hammurabi, the exalted prince, the worshiper of the gods, to cause justice to prevail in the land, to destroy the wicked and the evil, to prevent the strong from oppressing the weak, to go forth like the Sun over the Black Head Race, to enlighten the land and to further the welfare of the people. Hammurabi, the governor named by Bel, am I, who brought about plenty and abundance; who made everything for Nippur and Durilu complete; the exalted supporter of E-kur; the wise king, who restored Eridu to its place; who purified the sanctuary of E-apsu; who stormed the four quarters of the world; who made the fame of Babylon great; who rejoiced the heart of Marduk, his lord; who daily served in Esagila; of the seed royal, which Sin begat; who filled the city of Ur with plenty; the pious and suppliant one, who brought abundance to E-gis-sir-gal; the diplomatic king, obedient to the mighty Shamash; who refounded Sippar; who clothed with green the shrines of Malkat; who decorated E-babbara, which is like a heavenly dwelling; the warrior, the protector of Larsa; who rebuilt E-babbara for Shamash, his helper; the lord, who gave life to the city of Uruk; who supplied water in abundance to its inhabitants; who raised the turrets of Eanna; who brought riches to Anu and Nana; the divine protector of the land; who collected the scattered people of Nisin; who supplied E-gal-mah with luxurious abundance; the monarch, the city king, the brother of Za-ma-ma; who laid the foundations of the settlement of Kish; who surrounded E-te-me-ur-sag with splendor; who constructed the great shrines of Nana; the patron of the temple of Har-sag-kalama, the grave of the enemy; whose help brings victory; who extended the limits of Cutha; who enlarged Shidlam in every way; the mighty bull, who gores the enemy; the beloved of Tu-tu; who made the city of Borsippa beautiful; the exalted one who was untiring for the welfare of Ezida; the divine city king, wise and intelligent, who extended the settlements of Dilbat; who stored up grain for the mighty Urash; the lord adorned with scepter and crown, whom the wise god Ma-ma has clothed with complete power; who defined the confines of Kish; who made sumptuous the splendid banquets in honor of Nin-tu; the wise and perfect one, who determined the pasture and watering places for Shir-pur-la (Lagash) and Girsu; who provided large sacrifices for the Temple of Fifty; who seized the enemy; the favorite of the exalted god (oracle); who put into execution the laws of Aleppo; who makes joyful the heart of Anunit; the illustrious prince, the lifting up of whose hands Adad recognizes; who pacifies the heart of Adad, the warrior, in Karkar; who re-established the appointments of E-ud-gal-gal; the king who gave life to Ud-nun-ki; the benefactor of the temple E-mah; the presented life to the city of Mashkan-shabri; who poured out abundance over Shid-lam; the wise governor, who captured the bandit caves (?), who provided a hiding-place for the people of Malka in their misfortune; who founded dwelling-places for them in plenty; who determined for all time the splendid sacrifices for Ea and Damgal-nunna, who had extended his dominion; the city king first in rank; who subdued the settlements along the Euphrates; the warrior of Dagan, his creator; who protected the people of Mera and Tutul; the exalted prince, who makes the face of Nana to shine; who established splendid banquets for Nin-a-zu; who helps his people in time of need; who establishes in security their property in Babylon; the governor of the people, the servant, whose deeds are pleasing to Anunit; who installed Anunit in E-ul-mash in Agane broadway; who made justice prevail and who ruled the race with right; who returned to Ashur its gracious protecting deity; who made the rising sun (?) to shine brilliantly; the king who made the name of Nana glorious in E-mish-mish in Nineveh: the exalted one, who makes supplication to the great gods; the descendant of Sumulailu, the powerful son of Sinmu-ballit, the ancient seed of royalty, the powerful king, the Sun of Babylon, who caused light to go forth over the lands of Sumer and Akkad; the king, who caused the four quarters of the world to render obedience; the favorite of Nana, am I. When Mardul sent me to rule the people and to bring help to the country, I established law and justice in the land and promoted the welfare of the people.

The Code of Hammurabi

1. If a man bring an accusation against a man, and charge him with a (capital) crime, but cannot prove it, he, the accuser, shall be put to death.

2. If a man charge a man with sorcery, and cannot prove it, he who is charged with sorcery shall go to the river, into the river he shall throw himself and if the river overcome him, his accuser shall take to himself his house (estate). If the river show that man to be innocent and he come forth unharmed, he who charged him with sorcery shall be put to death. He who threw himself into the river shall take to himself the house of his accuser.

3. If a man, in a case (pending judgment), bear false (threatening) witness, or do not establish the testimony that he has given, if that case be a case involving life, that man shall be put to death.

4. If a man (in a case) bear witness for grain or money (as a bribe), he shall himself bear the penalty imposed in that case.

5. If a judge pronounce a judgment, render a decision, deliver a

verdict duly signed and sealed and afterward alter his judgment, they shall call that judge to account for the alteration of the judgment which he had pronounced, and he shall pay twelve-fold the penalty which was in said judgment; and, in the assembly, they shall expel him from his seat of judgment, and he shall not return, and with the judges in a case he shall not take his seat.

6. If a man steal the property of a god (temple) or palace, that man shall be put to death; and he who receives from his hand the stolen (property) shall also be put to death.

7. If a man purchase silver or gold, manservant or maid servant, ox, sheep or ass, or anything else from a man's son, or a man's servant without witnesses or contracts, or if he receive (the same) in trust, that man shall be put to death as a thief.

8. If a man steal ox or sheep, ass or pig, or boat—if it be from a god (temple) or a palace, he shall restore thirtyfold; if it be from a freeman, he shall render tenfold. If the thief have nothing wherewith to pay he shall be put to death.

9. If a man, who has lost anything, find that which was lost in the possession of (another) man; and the man in whose possession the lost property is found say: "It was sold to me. I purchased it in the presence of witnesses:" and the owner of the lost property say: "I will bring witnesses to identify my lost property": if the purchaser produce the seller who has sold it to him and the witnesses in whose presence he purchased it, and the owner of the lost property produce witnesses to identify his lost property, the judges shall consider their evidence. The witnesses in whose presence the purchase was made and the witnesses to identify the lost property shall give their testimony in the presence of god. The seller shall be put to death as a thief; the owner of the lost property shall recover his loss; the purchaser shall recover from the estate of the seller the money which he paid out.

10. If the purchaser do not produce the seller who sold it to him, and the witnesses in whose presence he purchased it (and) if the owner of the lost property produce witnesses to identify his lost property, the purchaser shall be put to death as a thief; the owner of the lost property shall recover his loss.

11. If the owner (claimant) of the lost property do not produce

witnesses to identify his lost property, he has attempted fraud (has lied), he has stirred up strife (calumny), he shall be put to death.

12. If the seller have gone to (his) fate (*i.e.*, have died), the purchaser shall recover damages in said case fivefold from the estate of the seller.

13. If the witnesses of that man be not at hand, the judges shall declare a postponement for six months; and if he do not bring in his witnesses within the six months, that man has attempted fraud, he shall bear the penalty imposed in that case.

14. If a man steal a man's son, who is a minor, he shall be put to death.

15. If a man aid a male or female slave of the palace, or a male or female slave of a freeman to escape from the city gate, he shall be put to death.

16. If a man harbor in his house a male or female slave who has fled from the palace or from a freeman, and do not bring him (the slave) forth at the call of the commandment, the owner of that house shall be put to death.

17. If a man seize a male or female slave, a fugitive, in the field and bring that (slave) back to his owner, the owner of the slave shall pay him two shekels of silver.

18. If that slave will not name his owner, he shall bring him to the palace and they shall inquire into his antecedents and they shall return him to his owner.

19. If he detain that slave in his house and later the slave be found in his possession, that man shall be put to death.

20. If the slave escape from the hand of his captor, that man shall so declare, in the name of god, to the owner of the slave and shall go free.

21. If a man make a breach in a house, they shall put him to death in front of that breach and they shall thrust him therein.

22. If a man practice brigandage and be captured, that man shall be put to death.

23. If the brigand be not captured, the man who has been robbed, shall, in the presence of god, make an itemized statement of his loss, and the city and the governor, in whose province and jurisdiction the

robbery was committed, shall compensate him for whatever was lost.

24. If it be a life (that is lost), the city and governor shall pay one mana of silver to his heirs.

25. If a fire break out in a man's house and a man who goes to extinguish it casts his eye on the furniture of the owner of the house, and take the furniture of the owner of the house, that man shall be thrown into that fire.

26. If either an officer or a constable, who is ordered to go on an errand of the king, do not go but hire a substitute and dispatch him in his stead, that officer or constable shall be put to death; his hired substitute shall take to himself his (the officer's) house.

27. If an officer or a constable, who is in a garrison of the king, be captured, and afterward they give his field and garden to another and he conduct his business—if the former return and arrive in his city, they shall restore to him his field and garden and he himself shall conduct his business.

28. If an officer or a constable, who is in a fortress of the king, be captured (and) his son be able to conduct the business, they shall give to him the field and garden and he shall conduct the business of his father.

29. If his son be too young and be not able to conduct the business of his father, they shall give one-third of the field and of the garden to his mother, and his mother shall rear him.

30. If an officer or a constable from the beginning of (or, on account of) (his) business neglect his field, his garden, and his house and leave them uncared for (and) another after him take his field, his garden, and his house, and conduct his business for three years; if the former return and desire (or, would manage) his field, his garden, and his house, they shall not give them to him; he, who has taken (them) and conducted the business shall continue (to do so).

31. If he leave (them) uncared for but one year and return, they shall give him his field, his garden, and his house, and he himself shall continue his business.

32. If a merchant ransom either an officer or a constable who has been captured on an errand of the king, and enable him to reach his city; if there be sufficient ransom in his house, he shall ransom

himself: if there be not sufficient ransom in his house, in the temple of his city he shall be ransomed; if there be not sufficient ransom in the temple of his city, the palace shall ransom him. In no case shall his field or his garden or his house be given for his ransom.

33. If a governor or a magistrate take possession of the men of levy (or, pardon a deserter) or accept and send a hired substitute on an errand of the king, that governor or magistrate shall be put to death.

34. If a governor or a magistrate take the property of an officer, plunder an officer, let an officer for hire, present an officer in a judgment to a man of influence, take the gift which the king has given to an officer, that governor or magistrate shall be put to death.

35. If a man buy from an officer the cattle of sheep which the king has given to that officer, he shall forfeit his money.

36. In no case shall one sell the field or garden or house of an officer, constable or tax-gatherer.

37. If a man purchase the field or garden or house of an officer, constable or tax-gatherer, his deed-tablet shall be broken (canceled) and he shall forfeit his money and he shall return the field, garden or house to its owner.

38. An officer, constable or tax-gatherer shall not deed to his wife or daughter the field, garden or house, which is his business (*i.e.*, which is his by virtue of his office), nor shall he assign them for debt.

39. He may deed to his wife or daughter the field, garden or house which he has purchased and (hence) possesses, or he may assign them for debt.

40. A woman, merchant or other property-owner may sell field, garden or house. The purchaser shall conduct the business of the field, garden or house which he has purchased.

41. If a man have bargained for the field, garden or house of an officer, constable or tax-gatherer and given sureties, the officer, constable or tax-gatherer shall return to his field, garden or house and he shall take to himself the sureties which were given to him.

42. If a man rent a field for cultivation and do not produce any grain in the field, they shall call him to account, because he has not performed the work required on the field, and he shall give to the owner of the field grain on the basis of the adjacent (fields).

43. If he do not cultivate the field and neglect it, he shall give to the owner of the field grain on the basis of the adjacent (fields); and the field which he has neglected, he shall break up with hoes, he shall harrow and he shall return to the owner of the field.

44. If a man rent an unreclaimed field for three years to develop it, and neglect it and do not develop the field, in the fourth year he shall break up the field with hoes, he shall hoe and harrow it and he shall return it to the owner of the field and shall measure out ten GUR of grain per ten GAN.

45. If a man rent his field to a tenant for crop-rent and receive the crop-rent of his field and later Adad (*i.e.*, the Storm God) inundate the field and carry away the produce, the loss (falls on) the tenant.

46. If he have not received the rent of his field and he have rented the field for either one-half or one-third (of the crop), the tenant and the owner of the field shall divide the grain which is in the field according to agreement.

47. If the tenant give the cultivation of the field to the charge of another—because in a former year he has not gained a maintenance—the owner of the field shall not interfere. He would cultivate it, and his field has been cultivated and at the time of harvest he shall take grain according to his contracts.

48. If a man owe a debt and Adad inundate his field and carry away the produce, or, through lack of water, grain have not grown in the field, in that year he shall not make any return of grain to his creditor, he shall alter his contract-tablet and he shall not pay the interest for that year.

49. If a man obtain money from a merchant and give (as security) to the merchant a field to be planted with grain and sesame (and) say to him: "Cultivate the field, and take to thyself the grain and sesame which is produced;" if the tenant raise grain and sesame in the field, at the time of harvest, the owner of the field shall receive the grain and sesame which is in the field and he shall give to the merchant grain for the loan which he had obtained from him and for the interest and for the maintenance of the tenant.

50. If he give (as security) a field planted with [grain] or a field planted with sesame, the owner of the field shall receive the grain or

the sesame which is in the field and he shall return the loan and its interest to the merchant.

51. If he have not the money to return, he shall give to the merchant [grain or] sesame, at their market value according to the scale fixed by the king, for the loan and its interest which he has obtained from the merchant.

52. If the tenant do not secure a crop of grain or sesame in his field, he shall not cancel his contract.

53. If a man neglect to strengthen his dyke and do not strengthen it, and a break be made in his dyke and the water carry away the farm-land, the man in whose dyke the break has been made shall restore the grain which he has damaged.

54. If he be not able to restore the grain, they shall sell him and his goods, and the farmer whose grain the water has carried away shall share (the results of the sale).

55. If a man open his canal for irrigation and neglect it and the water carry away an adjacent field, he shall measure out grain on the basis of the adjacent fields.

56. If a man open up the water and the water carry away the improvements of an adjacent field, he shall measure out ten GUR of grain per GAN.

57. If a shepherd have not come to agreement with the owner of a field to pasture his sheep on the grass; and if he pasture his sheep on the field without the consent of the owner, the owner of the field shall harvest his field, and the shepherd who has pastured his sheep on the field without the consent of the owner of the field, shall give over and above twenty GUR of grain per ten GAN to the owner of the field.

58. If, after the sheep have gone up from the meadow and have crowded their way out (?) of the gate into the public common, the shepherd turn the sheep into the field, and pasture the sheep on the field, the shepherd shall oversee the field on which he pastures and at the time of harvest he shall measure out sixty GUR of grain per ten GAN to the owner of the field.

59. If a man cut down a tree in a man's orchard, without the consent of the owner of the orchard, he shall pay one-half mana of silver.

60. If a man give a field to a gardener to plant as an orchard and the gardener plant the orchard and care for the orchard four years, in the fifth year the owner of the orchard and the gardener shall share equally; the owner of the orchard shall mark off his portion and take it.

61. If the gardener do not plant the whole field, but leave a space waste, they shall assign the waste space to his portion.

62. If he do not plant as an orchard the field which was given to him, if corn be the produce of the field, for the years during which it has been neglected, the gardener shall measure out to the owner of the field (such produce) on the basis of the adjacent fields, and he shall perform the required work on the field and he shall restore it to the owner of the field.

63. If the field be unreclaimed, he shall perform the required work on the field and he shall restore it to the owner of the field and he shall measure out ten GUR of grain per ten GAN for each year.

64. If a man give his orchard to a gardener to manage, the gardener shall give to the owner of the orchard two-thirds of the produce of the orchard, as long as he is in possession of the orchard; he himself shall take one-third.

65. If the gardener do not properly manage the orchard and he diminish the produce, the gardener shall measure out the produce of the orchard on the basis of the adjacent orchards.

100. ... he shall write down the interest on the money, as much as he has obtained, and he shall reckon its days and he shall make returns to his merchant.

101. If he do not meet with success where he goes, the agent shall double the amount of money obtained and he shall pay it to the merchant.

102. If a merchant give money to an agent as a favor, and the latter meet with a reverse where he goes, he shall return the principal of the money to the merchant.

103. If, when he goes on a journey, an enemy rob him of whatever he was carrying, the agent shall take an oath in the name of god and go free.

104. If a merchant give to an agent grain, wool, oil or goods of any kind with which to trade, the agent shall write down the value

and return (the money) to the merchant. The agent shall take a sealed receipt for the money which he gives to the merchant.

105. If the agent be careless and do not take a receipt for the money which he has given to the merchant, the money not receipted for shall not be placed to his account.

106. If an agent obtain money from a merchant and have a dispute with the merchant (*i.e.*, deny the fact), that merchant shall call the agent to account in the presence of god and witnesses for the money obtained and the agent shall give to the merchant threefold the amount of money which he obtained.

107. If a merchant lend to an agent and the agent return to the merchant whatever the merchant had given him; and if the merchant deny (receiving) what the agent has given to him, that agent shall call the merchant to account in the presence of god and witnesses and the merchant, because he has had a dispute with his agent, shall give to him sixfold the amount which he has obtained.

108. If a wine-seller do not receive grain as the price of drink, but if she receive money by the great stone, or make the measure for drink smaller than the measure for corn, they shall call that wine-seller to account, and they shall throw her into the water.

109. If outlaws collect in the house of a wine-seller, and she do not arrest those outlaws and bring them to the palace, that wine-seller shall be put to death.

110. If a priestess who is not living in a MAL.GE.A., open a wine-shop or enter a wine-shop for a drink, they shall burn that woman.

111. If a wine-seller give 60 KA of drink ... on credit, at the time of the harvest she shall receive 50 KA of grain.

112. If a man be on a journey and he give silver, gold, stones or portable property to a man with a commission for transportation, and if that man do not deliver that which was to be transported where it was to be transported, but take it to himself, the owner of the transported goods shall call that man to account for the goods to be transported which he did not deliver, and that man shall deliver to the owner of the transported goods fivefold the amount which was given to him.

113. If a man hold a [debt of] grain or money against a man, and if he take grain without the consent of the owner from the heap or the

granary, they shall call that man to account for taking grain without the consent of the owner from the heap or the granary, and he shall return as much grain as he took, and he shall forfeit all that he has lent, whatever it be.

114. If a man do not hold a [debt of] grain or money against a man, and if he seize him for debt, for each seizure he shall pay one-third mana of silver.

115. If a man hold a [debt of] grain or money against a man, and he seize him for debt, and the one seized die in the house of the one who seized him, that case has no penalty.

116. If the one seized die of abuse or neglect in the house of him who seized him, the owner of the one seized shall call the merchant to account; and if it be a man's son [that he seized] they shall put his son to death; if it be a man's servant [that he seized] he shall pay one-third mana of silver and he shall forfeit whatever amount he had lent.

117. If a man be in debt and sell his wife, son or daughter, or bind them over to service, for three years they shall work in the house of their purchaser of master; in the fourth year they shall be given their freedom.

118. If he bind over to service a male or female slave, and if the merchant transfer or sell such slave, there is no cause for complaint.

119. If a man be in debt and he sell his maid servant who has borne him children, the owner of the maid servant (*i.e.*, the man in debt) shall repay the money which the merchant paid (him), and he shall ransom his maid servant.

120. If a man store his grain in bins in the house of another and an accident happen to the granary, or the owner of the house open a bin and take grain or he raise a dispute about (or deny) the amount of grain which was stored in his house, the owner of the grain shall declare his grain in the presence of god, and the owner of the house shall double the amount of grain which he took and restore it to the owner of the grain.

121. If a man store grain in the house of another, he shall pay storage at the rate of 5 KA of grain per GUR each year.

122. If a man give to another silver, gold or anything else on

deposit, whatever he gives he shall show to witnesses and he shall arrange the contracts and (then) he shall make the deposit.

123. If a man give on deposit without witnesses or contracts, and at the place of the deposit they dispute with him (*i.e.*, deny the deposit), that case has no penalty.

124. If a man give to another silver, gold or anything else on deposit in the presence of witnesses and the latter dispute with him (or deny it), they shall call that man to account and he shall double whatever he disputed and repay it.

125. If a man give anything of his on deposit, and at the place of deposit either by burglary or pillage he suffer loss in common with the owner of the house, the owner of the house who has been negligent and has lost what was given to him on deposit shall make good (the loss) and restore (it) to the owner of the goods; the owner of the house shall institute a search for what has been lost and take it from the thief.

126. If a man have not lost anything, but say that he has lost something, or if he file a claim for loss when nothing has been lost, he shall declare his (alleged) loss in the presence of god, and he shall double and pay for the (alleged) loss the amount for which he had made claim.

127. If a man point the finger at a priestess or the wife of another and cannot justify it, they shall drag that man before the judges and they shall brand his forehead.

128. If a man take a wife and do not arrange with her the (proper) contracts, that woman is not a (legal) wife.

129. If the wife of a man be taken in lying with another man, they shall bind them and throw them into the water. If the husband of the woman would save his wife, or if the king would save his male servant (he may).

130. If a man force the (betrothed) wife of another who has not known a male and is living in her father's house, and he lie in her bosom and they take him, that man shall be put to death and that woman shall go free.

131. If a man accuse his wife and she has not been taken in lying with another man, she shall take an oath in the name of god and she shall return to her house.

132. If the finger have been pointed at the wife of a man because of another man, and she have not been taken in lying with another man, for her husband's sake she shall throw herself into the river.

133. If a man be captured and there be maintenance in his house and his wife go out of her house, she shall protect her body and she shall not enter into another house.

133A. [If] that woman do not protect her body and enter into another house, they shall call that woman into account and they shall throw her into the water.

134. If a man be captured and there no be maintenance in his house and his wife enter into another house, that woman has no blame.

135. If a man be captured and there no be maintenance in his house and his wife enter openly into another house and bear children; if later her husband return and arrive in his city, that woman shall return to her husband (and) the children shall go to their father.

136. If a man desert his city and flee and afterwards his wife enter into another house; if that man return and would take his wife, the wife of the fugitive shall not return to her husband because he hated his city and fled.

137. If a man set his face to put away a concubine who has borne him children or a wife who has presented him with children, he shall return to that woman her dowry and shall give to he the income of field, garden and goods and she shall bring up her children; from the time that her children are grown up, from whatever is given to her children they shall give to her a portion corresponding to that of a son and the man of her choice may marry her.

138. If a man would put away his wife who has not borne him children, he shall give her money to the amount of her marriage settlement and he shall make good to her the dowry which she brought from her father's house and then he may put her away.

139. If there were no marriage settlement, he shall give to her one mana of silver for a divorce.

140. If he be a freeman, he shall give her one-third mana of silver.

141. If the wife of a man who is living in his house, set her face to go out and play the part of a fool, neglect her house, belittle her

husband, they shall call her to account: if her husband say: "I have put her away," he shall let her go. On her departure nothing shall be given to her for her divorce. If her husband say: "I have not put her away," her husband may take another woman. The first woman shall dwell in the house of her husband as a maid servant.

142. If a woman hate her husband, and say: "thou shalt not have me," they shall inquire into her antecedents for her defects; and if she have been a careful mistress and been without reproach and her husband has been going about and greatly belittling her, that woman has no blame. She shall receive her dowry and go to her father's house.

143. If she have not been a careful mistress, have gadded about, have neglected her house and have belittled her husband, they shall throw that woman into the water.

144. If a man take a wife and that wife give a maid servant to her husband and she bear children; if that man set his face to take a concubine, they shall not countenance him. He may not take a concubine.

145. If a man take a wife and she do not present him with children and he set his face to take a concubine, that man may take a concubine and bring her into his house. That concubine shall not rank with his wife.

146. If a man take a wife and she give a maid servant to her husband, and that maid servant bear children and afterwards would take rank with her mistress; because she has borne children, her mistress may not sell her for money, but she may reduce her to bondage and count her among the maid servants.

147. If she have not borne children, her mistress may sell her for money.

148. If a man take a wife and she become afflicted with disease, and if he set his face to take another, he may. His wife, who is afflicted with disease, he shall not put away. She shall remain in the house which he has built and he shall maintain her as long as she lives.

149. If that woman do not elect to remain in her husband's house, he shall make good to her the dowry which she brought from her father's house and she may go.

150. If a man give to his wife field, garden, house or goods and he deliver to her a sealed deed, after (the death of) her husband, her children cannot make claim against her. The mother after her (death) may will to her child whom she loves, but to a brother she may not.

151. If a woman, who dwells in the house of a man, make a contract with her husband that a creditor of his may not hold her (for his debts) and compel him to deliver a written agreement; if that man were in debt before he took that woman, his creditor may not hold his wife, and if that woman were in debt before she entered the house of that man, her creditor may not hold her husband.

152. If they contract a debt after the woman has entered into the house of the man, both of them shall be answerable to the merchant.

153. If a woman bring about the death of her husband for the sake of another man, they shall impale her.

154. If a man have known his daughter, they shall expel that man from the city.

155. If a man have betrothed a bride to his son and his son have known her, and if he (the father) afterward lie in her bosom and they take him, they shall bind that man and throw him in the water.

156. If a man have betrothed a bride to his son and his son have not known her but he himself lie in her bosom, he shall pay her one-half mana of silver and he shall make good to her whatever she brought from the house of her father and the man of her choice may take her.

157. If a man lie in the bosom of his mother after (the death of) his father, they shall burn both of them.

158. If a man, after the death (of his father), be taken in the bosom of the chief wife (of his father) who has borne children, that man shall be cut off from his father's house.

159. If a man, who has brought a present to the house of his father-in-law and has given the marriage settlement, look with longing upon another woman and say to his father-in-law, "I will not take thy daughter;" the father of the daughter shall take to himself whatever was brought to him.

160. If a man bring a present to the house of his father-in-law and give a marriage settlement and the father of the daughter say, "I

will not give thee my daughter;" he (*i.e.*, the father-in-law) shall double the amount which was brought to him and return it.

161. If a man bring a present to the house of his father-in-law and give a marriage settlement, and his friend slander him; and if his father-in-law say to the claimant for the wife, "My daughter thou shalt not have," he (the father-in-law) shall double the amount which was brought to him and return it, but his friend may not have his wife.

162. If a man take a wife and she bear him children and that woman die, her father may not lay claim to her dowry. Her dowry belongs to her children.

163. If a man take a wife and she do not present him with children and that woman die; if his father-in-law return to him the marriage settlement which that man brought to the house of his father-in-law, her husband may not lay claim to the dowry of that woman. Her dowry belongs to the house of her father.

164. If his father-in-law do not return to him the marriage settlement, he may deduct from her dowry the amount of the marriage settlement and return (the rest) of her dowry to the house of her father.

165. If a man present field, garden or house to his favorite son and write for him a sealed deed; after the father dies, when the brothers divide, he shall take the present which the father gave him, and over and above they shall divide the goods of the father's house equally.

166. If a man take wives for his sons and do not take a wife for his youngest son, after the father dies, when the brothers divide, he shall take the present which the father gave him, and over and above they shall divide the goods of the father's house equally.

167. If a man take a wife and she bear him children and that woman die, and after her (death) he take another wife and she bear him children and later the father die, the children of the mothers shall not divide (the estate). They shall receive the dowries of the respective mothers and divide equally the goods of the house of the father.

168. If a man set his face to disinherit his son and say to the judges: "I will disinherit my son," the judges shall inquire into his antecedents, and if the son have not committed a crime sufficiently

grave to cut him off from sonship, the father may not cut off his son from sonship.

169. If he have committed a crime against his father sufficiently grave to cut him off from sonship, they shall condone his first (offense). If he commit a crime a second time, the father may cut off his son from sonship.

170. If a man's wife bear him children and his maid servant bear him children, and the father during his lifetime say to the children which the maid servant bore him: "My children," and reckon them with the children of his wife, after the father dies the children of the wife and the children of the maid servant shall divide the goods of the father's house equally. The child of the wife shall have the right of choice at the division.

171. But if a father during his lifetime have not said to the children which the maid servant bore him: "My children;" after the father dies, the children of the maid servant shall not share in the goods of the father's house with the children of the wife. The maid servant and her children shall be given their freedom. The children of the wife may not lay claim to the children of the maid servant for service. The wife shall receive her dowry and the gift which her husband gave and deeded to her on a tablet and she may dwell in the house of her husband and enjoy (the property) as long as she lives. She cannot sell it, however, for after her (death) it belongs to her children.

172. If her husband have not given her a gift, they shall make good her dowry and she shall receive the goods of her husband's house a portion corresponding to that of a son. If her children scheme to drive her out of the house, the judges shall inquire into her antecedents and if the children be in the wrong, she shall not go out from her husband's house. If the woman set her face to go out, she shall leave to her children the gift which her husband gave her; and she shall receive the dowry of her father's house, and the husband of her choice may take her.

173. If that woman bear children to her later husband into whose house she has entered and later on that woman die, the former and the later children shall divide her dowry.

174. If she do not bear children to her later husband, the children of her first husband shall receive her dowry.

175. If either a slave of the palace or a slave of the freeman take the daughter of a man (gentleman) and she bear children, the owner of the slave may not lay claim to the children of the daughter of the man for service.

176. And if a slave of the palace or a slave of the freeman take the daughter of a man (gentleman); and if, when he takes her, she enter into the house of the slave of the palace or the slave of the freeman with the dowry of her father's house; if from the time that they join hands, they build a house and acquire property; and if later on the slave of the palace or the slave of the freeman die, the daughter of the man shall receive her dowry, and they shall divide into two parts whatever her husband and she had acquired from the time they joined hands; the owner of the slave shall receive one-half and the daughter of the man shall receive one-half for her children.

176A. If the daughter of a man had no dowry they shall divide into two parts whatever her husband and she had acquired from the time they joined hands. The owner of the slave shall receive one-half and the daughter of the man shall receive one-half for her children.

177. If a widow, whose children are minors set her face to enter another house, she cannot do so without the consent of the judges. When she enters another house, the judges shall inquire into the state of her former husband and they shall intrust the estate of the former husband to the later husband and that woman, and they shall deliver to them a tablet (to sign). They shall administer the estate and rear the minors. They may not sell the household goods. He who purchases household goods belonging to the sons of a widow shall forfeit his money. The goods shall revert to the owner.

178. If (there be) a priestess or a devotee to whom her father has given a dowry or written a deed of gift; if in the deed which he has written for her, he have not written: "after her (death) she may give to whomsoever she may please," and if he have not granted her full discretion; after her father dies her brothers shall take her field and garden and they shall give her grain, oil and wool according to the value of her share and they shall make her content. If her brothers do not give her

grain, oil and wool according to the value of her share and they do not make her content, she may give her field and garden to any tenant she may please and her tenant shall maintain her. She shall enjoy the field, garden or anything else which her father gave her as long as she lives. She may not sell it, nor transfer it. Her heritage belongs to her brothers.

179. If (there be) a priestess or a devotee to whom her father has given a dowry or written a deed of gift; if in the deed which he has written for her, he have written "after her (death) she may give to whomsoever she may please," and he have granted her full discretion; after her father dies she may give it to whomsoever she may please after her (death). Her brothers may not lay claim against her.

180. If a father do not give a dowry to his daughter, a bride or devotee, after her father dies she shall receive as her share in the goods of her father's house the portion of a son and she shall enjoy it as long as she lives. After her (death), it belongs to her brothers.

181. If a father devote a votary or NU.PAR. to a god and do not give her a dowry, after her father dies she shall receive as her share in the goods of her father's house one-third of the portion of a son and she shall enjoy it as long as she lives. After her (death), it belongs to her brothers.

182. If a man do not give a dowry to his daughter, a priestess of Marduk of Babylon, and do not write for her a deed of gift; after her father dies she shall receive as her share with her brothers one-third the portion of a son in the goods of her father's house, but she shall not conduct the business thereof. A priestess of Marduk, after her (death), may give to whomsoever she may please.

183. If a father present a dowry to his daughter, who is a concubine, and give her to a husband and write a deed of gift; after the father dies she shall not share in the goods of her father's house.

184. If a man do not present a dowry to his daughter, who is a concubine, and do not give her to a husband; after her father dies her brothers shall present her a dowry proportionate to the fortune of her father's house and they shall give her to a husband.

185. If a man take in his name a young child as a son and rear him, one may not bring claim for that adopted son.

186. If a man take a young child as a son and, when he takes him,

he is rebellious toward his father and his mother (who have adopted him), that adopted son shall return to the house of his father.

187. One may not bring claim for the son of a NER.SE.GA. who is a palace guard, or the son of a devotee.

188. If an artisan take a son for adoption and teach him his handicraft, one may not bring claim for him.

189. If he do not teach him his handicraft, that adopted son may return to his father's house.

190. If a man do not reckon among his sons the young child whom he has taken and reared, that adopted son may return to his father's house.

191. If a man, who has taken a young child as a son and reared him, establish his own house and acquire children, and set his face to cut off the adopted son, that son shall not go his way. The father who reared him shall give to him of his goods one-third the portion of a son and he shall go. He shall not give to him of field, garden or house.

192. If the son of a NER.SE.GA. or the son of a devotee say to his father who has reared him or his mother who has reared him: "My father thou art not," "My mother thou art not," they shall cut out his tongue.

193. If the son of a NER.SE.GA. or the son of a devotee identify his own father's house and hate the father that has reared him and the mother who has reared him and go back to his father's house, they shall pluck out his eye.

194. If man give his son to a nurse and that son die in the hands of the nurse, and the nurse substitute another son without the consent of his father or mother, they shall call her to account, and because she has substituted another son without the consent of his father or mother, they shall cut off his breast.

195. If a son strike his father, they shall cut off his fingers.

196. If a man destroy the eye of another man, they shall destroy his eye.

197. If one break a man's bone, they shall break his bone.

198. If one destroy the eye of a freeman or break the bone of a freeman he shall pay one mana of silver.

199. If one destroy the eye of a man's slave or break a bone of a man's slave he shall pay one-half his price.

200. If a man knock out a tooth of a man of his own rank, they shall knock out his tooth.

201. If one knock out a tooth of a freeman, he shall pay one-third mana of silver.

202. If a man strike the person of a man (*i.e.*, commit an assault) who is his superior, he shall receive sixty strokes with an ox-tail whip in public.

203. If a man strike another man on his own rank, he shall pay one mana of silver.

204. If a freeman strike a freeman, he shall pay ten shekels of silver.

205. If a man's slave strike a man's son, they shall cut off his ear.

206. If a man strike another man in a quarrel and wound him, he shall swear: "I struck him without intent," and he shall be responsible for the physician.

207. If (he) die as a result of the stroke, he shall swear (as above), and if he be a man, he shall pay one-half mana of silver.

208. If (he) be a freeman, he shall pay one-third mana of silver.

209. If a man strike a man's daughter and bring about a miscarriage, he shall pay ten shekels of silver for her miscarriage.

210. If that woman die, they shall put his daughter to death.

211. If, through a stroke, he bring about a miscarriage to the daughter of a freeman, he shall pay five shekels of silver.

212. If that woman die, he shall pay one-half mana of silver.

213. If he strike the female slave of a man and bring about a miscarriage, he shall pay two shekels of silver.

214. If that female slave die, he shall pay one-third mana of silver.

215. If a physician operate on a man for a severe wound (or make a severe wound upon a man) with a bronze lancet and save the man's life; or if he open an abscess (in the eye) of a man with a bronze lancet and save that man's eye, he shall receive ten shekels of silver (as his fee).

216. If he be a freeman, he shall receive five shekels.

217. If it be a man's slave, the owner of the slave shall give two shekels of silver to the physician.

218. If a physician operate on a man for a severe wound with a bronze lancet and cause that man's death; or open an abscess (in the

eye) of a man with a bronze lancet and destroy the man's eye, they shall cut off his fingers.

219. If a physician operate on a slave of a freeman for a severe wound with a bronze lancet and cause his death, he shall restore a slave of equal value.

220. If he open an abscess (in his eye) with a bronze lancet, and destroy his eye, he shall pay silver to extent of one-half of his price.

221. If a physician set a broken bone for a man or cure his diseased bowels, the patient shall give five shekels of silver to the physician.

222. If he be a freeman, he shall give three shekels of silver.

223. If it be a man's slave, the owner of the slave shall give two shekels of silver to the builder.

224. If a veterinary physician operate on an ox or an ass for a severe wound and save its life, the owner of the ox or ass shall give to the physician, as his fee, one-sixth of a shekel of silver.

225. If he operate on an ox or an ass for a severe wound and cause its death, he shall give to the owner of the ox or ass one-fourth its value.

226. If a brander, without the consent of the owner of the slave, brand a slave with the sign that he cannot be sold, they shall cut off the fingers of that brander.

227. If a man deceive a brander and he brand a slave with the sign that he cannot be sold, they shall put that man to death, and they shall cast him into his house. The brander shall swear: "I did not brand him knowingly," and he shall go free.

228. If a builder build a house for a man and complete it, (that man) shall give him two shekels of silver per SAR of house as his wage.

229. If a builder build a house for a man and do not make its construction firm, and the house which he has built collapse and cause the death of the owner of the house, that builder shall be put to death.

230. If it cause the death of a son of the owner of the house, they shall put to death a son of that builder.

231. If it cause the death of a slave of the owner of the house, he shall give the owner of the house a slave of equal value.

232. If it destroy property, he shall restore whatever it destroyed, and because he did not make the house which he built firm and it collapsed, he shall rebuild the house which collapsed from his own property (*i.e.*, at his own expense).

233. If a builder build a house for a man and do not make its construction meet the requirements and a wall fall in, that builder shall strengthen that wall at his own expense.

234. If a boatman build a boat of 60 GUR for a man, he shall give him 2 shekels of silver as his wage.

235. If a boatman build a boat for a man and he do not make its construction seaworthy and that boat meet with a disaster in the same year in which it was put into commission, the boatman shall reconstruct the boat and he shall strengthen it at his own expense and he shall give the boat when strengthened to the owner of the boat.

236. If a man hire his boat to a boatman and the boatman be careless and he sink or wreck the boat, the boatman shall replace the boat to the owner of the boat.

237. If a man hire a boatman and a boat and freight it with grain, wool, oil, dates or any other kind of freight, and that boatman is careless and he sink the boat or wreck its cargo, the boatman shall replace the boat which he sank and whatever portion of the cargo he wrecked.

238. If a boatman sink a man's boat and refloat it, he shall give silver to the extent of one-half its value.

239. If a man hire a boatman, he shall give him 6 GUR of grain per year.

240. If a boat under way strike a ferryboat (or, boat at anchor), and sink it, the owner of the boat whose boat was sunk shall make declaration in the presence of god of everything that was lost in his boat and (the owner) of (the vessel) under way which sank the ferryboat shall replace his boat and whatever was lost.

241. If a man seize an ox for debt, he shall pay one-third mana of silver.

242. 243. If a man hire (an ox) for a year, he shall give to its owner four GUR of grain as the hire of a draught ox, (and) three GUR of grain as the hire of an ox (?).

244. If a man hire an ox or an ass and a lion kill it in the field, it is the owner's affair.

245. If a man hire an ox and cause its death through neglect or abuse, he shall restore an ox of equal value to the owner of the ox.

246. If a man hire an ox and he break its foot or cut its hamstring (?), he shall restore an ox of equal value to the owner of the ox.

247. If a man hire an ox and destroy its eye, he shall pay silver to the owner of the ox to the extent of one-half its value.

248. If a man hire an ox and break its horn or cut off its tail or injure the flesh (through which) the ring (passes), he shall pay silver to the owner of the ox to the extent of one-quarter its value.

249. If a man hire an ox and a god strike it and it die, the man who hired the ox shall take an oath before god and go free.

250. If a bull, when passing through the street, gore a man and bring about his death, this case has no penalty.

251. If a man's bull have been wont to gore and they have made known to him his habit of goring, and he have not protected his horns or have not tied him up, and that bull gore the son of a man and bring about his death, he shall pay one-half mana of silver.

252. If it be the servant of a man, he shall pay one-third mana of silver.

253. If a man hire a man to oversee his farm and to furnish him the seed-grain and intrust him with oxen and contract with him to cultivate the field, and that man steal either the seed or the crop and it be found in his possession, they shall cut off his fingers.

254. If he take the seed-grain and overwork the oxen, he shall restore the quantity of grain which he has hoed.

255. If he let the oxen of the man on hire, or steal the seed-grain and there be no crop in the field, they shall call that man to account and he shall measure out 60 GUR of grain per 10 GAN.

256. If he be not able to meet his obligation, they shall leave him in that field with the cattle.

257. If a man hire a field-laborer, he shall pay him 8 GUR of grain per year.

258. If a man hire a herdsman, he shall pay him 6 GUR of grain per year.

259. If a man steal a watering-machine in a field, he shall pay 5 shekels of silver to the owner of the watering-machine.

260. If a man steal a watering-bucket or a harrow, he shall pay 3 shekels of silver.

261. If a man hire a herdsman to pasture oxen or sheep, he shall pay him 8 GUR of grain per year.

262. If a man, an ox or a sheep to ...

263. If he lose an ox or sheep which is given to him, he shall restore to their owner ox for ox, sheep for sheep.

264. If a shepherd, to whom oxen or sheep have been given to pasture, receive as his hire whatever was agreed upon (?) and be satisfied, and he let the cattle or sheep decrease in number, or lessen the birth rate, according to his contracts he shall make good the birth rate and the produce.

265. If a shepherd, to whom oxen or sheep have been given to pasture, have been dishonest or have altered their price, or sold them, they shall call him to account, and he shall restore to their owner oxen or sheep tenfold what he has stolen.

266. If a visitation of god happen to a fold, or a lion kill, the shepherd shall declare himself innocent before god, and the owner of the fold shall suffer the damage.

267. If a shepherd be careless and he bring about an accident in the fold, the shepherd shall make good in cattle and sheep the loss through the accident which he brought about in the fold, and give them to the owner.

268. If a man hire an ox to thresh, 20 KA of grain is its hire.

269. If he hire an ass to thresh, 10 KA of grain is its hire.

270. If he hire a young animal (goat) to thresh, 1 KA of grain is its hire.

271. If a man hire oxen, a wagon and a driver, he shall pay 180 KA of grain per day.

272. If a man hire a wagon only, he shall pay 40 KA of grain per day.

273. If a man hire a laborer, from the beginning of the year until the fifth month, he shall pay 6 SE of silver per day; from the sixth month until the end of the year he shall pay 5 SE of silver per day.

274. If a man hire an artisan, the wage of a ... is 5 SE of silver; the

wage of a brickmaker (?) is 5 SE of silver; the wage of a tailor is 5 SE of silver; the wage of a ... is ... SE of silver; the wage of a ... is ... SE of silver; the wage of a ... is ... SE of silver; the wage of a carpenter is 4 SE of silver; the wage of a (?) is 4 SE of silver; the wage of a (?) is ... SE of silver; the wage of a mason is ... SE of silver; so much per day shall he pay.

275. If a man hire a ... its hire is 3 SE of silver per day.

276. If he hire a sail-boat (?), he shall pay 2½ SE of silver per day as its hire.

277. If a man hire a boat of sixty GUR (tonnage), he shall pay 1/6 of a shekel of silver as its hire per day.

278. If a man sell a male or female slave, and the slave have not completed his month, and the bennu fever fall upon him, he (the purchaser) shall return him to the seller and he shall receive the money which he paid.

279. If a man sell a male or female slave and there be a claim upon him, the seller shall be responsible for the claim.

280. If a man purchase a male or female slave of a man in a foreign country, and if, when he comes back to his own land, the (former) owner of the male or female slave recognize his male or female slave—if the male or female slave be a native of the land, he shall grant them their freedom without money.

281. If they be natives of another land, the purchaser shall declare before god the money which he paid (for them), and the owner of the male or female slave shall give to the merchant the money which he paid out, and he (the owner) shall receive into his care his male or female slave.

282. If a male slave say to his master: "Thou art not my master," his master shall prove him to be his slave and shall cut off his ear.

Epilogue

The righteous laws, which Hammurabi, the wise king, established and (by which) he gave the land stable support and pure government. Hammurabi, the perfect king, am I. I was not careless, nor was I neglectful of the Black-Head people, whose rule Bel presented and Marduk delivered to me. I provided them with a peaceful country. I opened up difficult barriers and lent them support. With the powerful weapon which Za-má-má and Nana entrusted to me, with the breadth of vision which Ea allotted me, with the might which Marduk gave me, I expelled the enemy to the North and South; I made an end of their raids; I brought health to the land; I made the populace to rest in security; I permitted no one to molest them.

The great gods proclaimed me and I am the guardian governor, whose scepter is righteous and whose beneficent protection is spread over my city. In my bosom I carried the people of the land of Sumer and Akkad; under my protection I brought their brethren into security; in my wisdom I restrained (hid) them; that the strong might not oppose the weak, and that they should give justice to the orphan and the widow, in Babylon, the city whose turrets Anu and Bel raised; in Esagila, the temple whose foundations are firm as heaven and earth, for the pronouncing of judgments in the land, for the rendering of decisions for the land, and for the righting of wrong, my weighty words I have written upon my monument, and in the presence of my image as king of righteousness have I established.

The king, who is pre-eminent among city kings, am I. My words are precious, my wisdom is unrivaled. By the command of Shamash, the great judge of heaven and earth, may I make righteousness to shine forth on the land. By the order of Marduk, my lord, may no one efface my statutes, may my name be remembered with favor in Esagila forever. Let any oppressed man, who has a cause, come before my image as king of righteousness! Let him read the inscription on my monument! Let him give heed to my weighty words! And may my monument enlighten him as to his cause and may he understand his case! May he set his heart at ease! (and he will exclaim): "Hammurabi indeed is a ruler who is like a real father to his people; he has given reverence to the words of Marduk, his lord; he has obtained victory for Marduk in North and South; he has made glad the heart of Marduk, his lord; he has established prosperity for the people for all time and given a pure government to the land." Let him read the code and pray with a full heart before Marduk, my lord, and Zarpanit, my lady, and may the protecting deities, the gods who enter Esagila, daily in the midst of Esagila look with favor on his wishes (plans) in the presence of Marduk, my lord, and Zarpanit, my lady!

In the days that are yet to come, for all future time, may the king who is in the land observe the words of righteousness which I have written upon my monument! May he not alter the judgments of the land which I have pronounced, or the decisions of the country which I have rendered! May he not efface my statues! If that man have wisdom, if he wish to give his land good government, let him give attention to the words which I have written upon my monument! And may this monument enlighten him as to procedure and administration, the judgments which I have pronounced, and the decisions which I have rendered for the land! And let him rightly rule his Black-Head people; let him pronounce judgments for them and render for them decisions! Let him root out the wicked and evildoer from his land! Let him promote the welfare of his people!

Hammurabi, the king of righteousness, whom Shamash has endowed with justice, am I. My words are weighty; my deeds are unrivaled *[...]* and the bringing to honor.

If that man pay attention to my words which I have written upon my monument, do not efface my judgments, do not overrule my words, and do not alter my statues, then will Shamash prolong that man's reign, as he has mine, who am king of righteousness, that he may rule his people in righteousness.

If that man do not pay attention to my words which I have written upon my monument; if he forget my curse and do not fear the curse of god; if he abolish the judgments which I have formulated, overrule my words, alter my statues, efface my name written thereon and write his own name; on account of these curses, commission another to do so—as for that man, be he king or lord, or priest-king or commoner, whoever he may be, may the great god, the father of the gods, who has ordained my reign, take from him the glory of his sovereignty, may he break his scepter, and curse his fate!

May Bel, the lord, who determines destinies, whose command cannot be altered, who has enlarged my dominion, drive him out from his dwelling through a revolt which his hand cannot control and a curse destructive to him. May he determine as his fate a reign of sighs, days few in number, years of famine, darkness without light, death staring him in the face! The destruction of his city, the dispersion of his people, the wresting away of his dominion, the blotting out of his name and memory from the land, may Bel order with his potent command!

May Belit, the august mother, whose command is potent in E-kur, who looks with gracious favor upon my plans, in the place of judgment and decisions pervert his words in the presence of Bel! May she put into the mouth of Bel, the king, the ruin of his land, the destruction of his people and the pouring out of his life like water!

May Ea, the great prince, whose decrees take precedence, the leader of the gods, who knows everything, who prolongs the days of my life, deprive him of knowledge and wisdom! May he bring him to oblivion, and dam up his rivers at their sources! May he not permit corn, which is the life of the people, to grow in his land!

May Shamash, the great judge of heaven and earth, who rules all living creatures, the lord (inspiring) confidence, overthrow his dominion; may he not grant him his rights! May he make him to err in his path, may he destroy the mass (foundation) of his troops! May he bring to his view an evil omen of the uprooting of the foundation of his sovereignty, and the ruin of his land.

May the blighting curse of Shamash come upon him quickly! May he cut off his life above (upon the earth)! Below, within the earth, may he deprive his spirit of water!

May Sin, the lord of heaven, my divine creator, whose scimetar shines among the gods, take away from him the crown and throne of sovereignty! May he lay upon him heavy guilt and great sin, which will not depart from him! May he bring to an end the days, months, and years of his reign with sighing and tears! May he multiply the burdens of his sovereignty! May he determine as his fate a life like unto death!

May Adad, the lord of abundance, the regent of heaven and earth, my helper, deprive him of the rain from heaven and the water-floods from the springs! May he bring his land to destruction through want and hunger! May he break loose furiously over his city and turn his land into a heap left by a whirlwind!

May Za-má-má, the great warrior, the chief son of E-kur, who goes at my right hand, shatter his weapons on the field of battle! May he turn day into night for him, and place his enemy over him!

May Ishtar, goddess of battle and conflict, who makes ready my weapons, the gracious protecting deity, who loves my reign, curse his dominion with great fury in her wrathful heart, and turn good into evil for him! May she shatter his weapons on the field of battle and conflict! May she create confusion and revolt for him! May she strike down his warriors, may their blood water the earth! May she cast the bodies of his warriors upon the fields in heaps! May she not grant his warriors (burial (?))! May she deliver him into the hands of his enemies, and may they carry him away bound into a hostile land!

May Nergal, the mighty among the gods, the warrior without an equal, who grants me victory, in his great power, burn his people like a raging fire of swamp-reed. With his powerful weapon, may he cut him off and may he break his members like an earthen image!

May Nin-tu, the exalted mistress of the lands, the mother who bore me, deny him a son! May she not let him hold a name among his people, nor beget an heir!

May Nin-kar-ra-ak, the daughter of Anu, who commands favors for me in E-kur, cause to come upon his members until it overcomes his life, a grievous malady, an evil disease, a dangerous sore, which cannot be cured, which the physician cannot diagnose, which he cannot allay with bandages, and which, like the bite of death, cannot be removed! May he lament the loss of his vigor!

May the great gods of heaven and earth, the Anunnaki in their assembly, curse with blighting curses the wall of the temple, the construction of this E-babbarra, his seed, his land, his army, his people, and his troops!

May Bel with his command which cannot be altered curse him with a powerful and may it come upon him speedily!

Copyright © 2024 by Alicia EDITIONS
Credits: www.canva.com; Alicia EDITIONS,
https://commons.wikimedia.org/wiki/File:Chaos_Monster_and_Sun_God.png
Prologue of the Code of Hammurabi (the 305 first inscripted squares on the stele).
Some gaps in the list of benefits bestowed on cities recently annexed by Hammurabi
may prove the tablet is older than the celebrated basalt stele (also in the Louvre).
https://commons.wikimedia.org/wiki/File:Prologue_Hammurabi_Code_Louvre_AO10237.jpg
Photo of the discovery of Hammurabi's code stele, 1901.
https://commons.wikimedia.org/wiki/File:Code_of_Hammurabi_104.jpg
A section of the Code of Hammurabi. Extracted from File:Code of Hammurabi
(1904).pdf (p. 225—226)
PAPERBACK:
E-BOOK:
HARDCOVER:
All rights reserved.
No part of this book may be reproduced in any form or by any electronic or mechanical
means, including information storage and retrieval systems, without written
permission from the author, except for the use of brief quotations in a book review.

www.ingramcontent.com/pod-product-compliance
Lightning Source LLC
LaVergne TN
LVHW032013070526
838202LV00059B/6433